The Seven Seas

By Rudyard Kipling

Author of Many Inventions,
Barrack-Room Ballads,
The Jungle Books,
Etc.

New York
D. Appleton and Company
1896

CONTENTS.

	PAGE
DEDICATION TO THE CITY OF BOMBAY	V
A SONG OF THE ENGLISH	I
THE FIRST CHANTEY	18
THE LAST CHANTEY	21
THE MERCHANTMEN	26
MCANDREW'S HYMN	31
THE MIRACLES	46
THE NATIVE-BORN	48
THE KING	54
THE RHYME OF THE THREE SEALERS	57
THE DERELICT	71
THE SONG OF THE BANJO	74
"THE LINER SHE'S A LADY"	80
MULHOLLAND'S CONTRACT	83
ANCHOR SONG	87
THE SEA-WIFE	90
HYMN BEFORE ACTION	93
TO THE TRUE ROMANCE	96
THE FLOWERS	100
THE LAST RHYME OF TRUE THOMAS	104

iv　　　　　　**Contents.**

	PAGE
THE STORY OF UNG	113
THE THREE-DECKER	118
AN AMERICAN	123
THE MARY GLOSTER	126
SESTINA OF THE TRAMP-ROYAL	141

BARRACK-ROOM BALLADS.

When 'Omer smote 'is bloomin' lyre.	144
"BACK TO THE ARMY AGAIN"	145
"BIRDS OF PREY" MARCH	149
"SOLDIER AN' SAILOR TOO"	152
SAPPERS	156
THAT DAY	160
"THE MEN THAT FOUGHT AT MINDEN"	163
CHOLERA CAMP	167
THE LADIES	171
BILL 'AWKINS	175
THE MOTHER-LODGE	177
"FOLLOW ME 'OME"	181
THE SERGEANT'S WEDDIN'	184
THE JACKET	187
THE 'EATHEN	191
THE SHUT-EYE SENTRY	198
"MARY, PITY WOMEN!"	202
FOR TO ADMIRE	205
L'ENVOI	208

DEDICATION
To The City Of Bombay.

THE Cities are full of pride,
   Challenging each to each—
This from her mountain-side,
   That from her burthened beach.

They count their ships full tale—
   Their corn and oil and wine,
Derrick and loom and bale,
   And rampart's gun-flecked line ;
City by city they hail :
   "Hast aught to match with mine?"

And the men that breed from them
   They traffic up and down,
But cling to their cities' hem
   As a child to the mother's gown.

When they talk with the stranger bands,
   Dazed and newly alone;
When they walk in the stranger lands,
   By roaring streets unknown;
Blessing her where she stands
   For strength above their own.

(On high to hold her fame
   That stands all fame beyond,
By oath to back the same,
   Most faithful-foolish-fond;
Making her mere-breathed name
   Their bond upon their bond.)

So thank I God my birth
   Fell not in isles aside—
Waste headlands of the earth,
   Or warring tribes untried—
But that she lent me worth
   And gave me right to pride.

Surely in toil or fray
   Under an alien sky,
Comfort it is to say:
   "Of no mean city am I."

(Neither by service nor fee
    Come I to mine estate—
Mother of Cities to me,
    For I was born in her gate,
Between the palms and the sea,
    Where the world-end steamers wait.)

Now for this debt I owe,
    And for her far-borne cheer
Must I make haste and go
    With tribute to her pier.

And she shall touch and remit
    After the use of kings
(Orderly, ancient, fit)
    My deep-sea plunderings,
And purchase in all lands.
    And this we do for a sign
    Her power is over mine,
And mine I hold at her hands.

A SONG OF THE ENGLISH.

Fair is our lot—O goodly is our heritage !
(Humble ye, my people, and be fearful in your
  mirth !)
  For the Lord our God Most High
  He hath made the deep as dry,
He hath smote for us a pathway to the ends of all
  the Earth !

Yea, though we sinned—and our rulers went from
  righteousness—
Deep in all dishonour though we stained our gar-
  ments' hem.
  Oh be ye not dismayed,
  Though we stumbled and we strayed,
We were led by evil counsellors—the Lord shall
  deal with them.

Hold ye the Faith — the Faith our Fathers
  sealèd us ;
Whoring not with visions—overwise and overstale.

1

Except ye pay the Lord
Single heart and single sword,
Of your children in their bondage shall He ask
them treble-tale.

Keep ye the Law—be swift in all obedience.
Clear the land of evil, drive the road and bridge
the ford.
Make ye sure to each his own
That he reap what he hath sown ;
By the peace among Our peoples let men know we
serve the Lord.

.　　.　　.　　.　　.　　.

Hear now a song—a song of broken interludes—
A song of little cunning ; of a singer nothing
worth.
Through the naked words and mean
May ye see the truth between
As the singer knew and touched it in the ends of
all the Earth !

The Coastwise Lights.

Our brows are wreathed with spindrift and the
    weed is on our knees;
Our loins are battered 'neath us by the swinging,
    smoking seas.
From reef and rock and skerry—over headland,
    ness and voe—
The Coastwise Lights of England watch the ships
    of England go!

Through the endless summer evenings, on the line-
    less, level floors;
Through the yelling Channel tempest when the
    syren hoots and roars—
By day the dipping house-flag and by night the
    rocket's trail—
As the sheep that graze behind us so we know
    them where they hail.

We bridge across the dark, and bid the helmsman
    have a care,
The flash that wheeling inland wakes his sleeping
    wife to prayer;

From our vexed eyries, head to gale, we bind in
    burning chains
The lover from the sea-rim drawn—his love in
    English lanes.

We greet the clippers wing-and-wing that race
    the Southern wool;
We warn the crawling cargo-tanks of Bremen,
    Leith and Hull;
To each and all our equal lamp at peril of the
    sea—
The white wall-sided warships or the whalers of
    Dundee!

Come up, come in from Eastward, from the guard-
    ports of the Morn !
Beat up, beat in from Southerly, O gipsies of the
    Horn!
Swift shuttles of an Empire's loom that weave us
    main to main,
The Coastwise Lights of England give you wel-
    come back again!

Go, get you gone up-Channel with the sea-crust
    on your plates;
Go, get you into London with the burden of your
    freights!

Haste, for they talk of Empire there, and say, if
    any seek,
The Lights of England sent you and by silence
    shall ye speak.

The Song of the Dead.

Hear now the Song of the Dead—in the North by
    the torn berg-edges—
They that look still to the Pole, asleep by their
    hide-stripped sledges.
Song of the Dead in the South—in the sun by their
    skeleton horses,
Where the warrigal whimpers and bays through
    the dust of the sere river-courses.

Song of the Dead in the East—in the heat-rotted
    jungle hollows,
Where the dog-ape barks in the kloof—in the brake
    of the buffalo-wallows.
Song of the Dead in the West—in the Barrens, the
    snow that betrayed them,
Where the wolverine tumbles their packs from the
    camp and the grave-mound they made them;
    Hear now the Song of the Dead!

I.

We were dreamers, dreaming greatly, in the man-
stifled town;

We yearned beyond the sky-line where the strange
roads go down.

Came the Whisper, came the Vision, came the
Power with the Need.

Till the Soul that is not man's soul was lent us to
lead.

As the deer breaks—as the steer breaks—from the
herd where they graze,

In the faith of little children we went on our
ways.

Then the wood failed—then the food failed—then
the last water dried—

In the faith of little children we lay down and
died.

On the sand-drift—on the veldt-side—in the fern-
scrub we lay,

That our sons might follow after by the bones on
the way.

Follow after—follow after! We have watered the
root,

And the bud has come to blossom that ripens for
fruit!

Follow after—we are waiting by the trails that
    we lost
For the sound of many footsteps, for the tread of a
    host.
Follow after—follow after—for the harvest is
    sown:
By the bones about the wayside ye shall come to
    your own!

When Drake went down to the Horn
    And England was crowned thereby,
'Twixt seas unsailed and shores unhailed
    Our Lodge—our Lodge was born
    (And England was crowned thereby).

Which never shall close again
    By day nor yet by night,
While man shall take his life to stake
    At risk of shoal or main
    (By day nor yet by night),

But standeth even so
    As now we witness here,
While men depart, of joyful heart,
    Adventure for to know.
    (As now bear witness here).

II.

We have fed our sea for a thousand years
    And she calls us, still unfed,
Though there's never a wave of all her waves
    But marks our English dead:
We have strawed our best to the weed's unrest
    To the shark and the sheering gull.
If blood be the price of admiralty,
    Lord God, we ha' paid in full!

There's never a flood goes shoreward now
    But lifts a keel we manned;
There's never an ebb goes seaward now
    But drops our dead on the sand—
But slinks our dead on the sands forlore,
    From The Ducies to the Swin.
If blood be the price of admiralty,
If blood be the price of admiralty,
    Lord God, we ha' paid it in!

We must feed our sea for a thousand years,
    For that is our doom and pride,
As it was when they sailed with the *Golden Hind*
    Or the wreck that struck last tide—
Or the wreck that lies on the spouting reef
    Where the ghastly blue-lights flare.

If blood be the price of admiralty,
If blood be the price of admiralty,
If blood be the price of admiralty,
    Lord God, we ha' bought it fair!

𝔗𝔥𝔢 𝔇𝔢𝔢𝔭-𝔰𝔢𝔞 ℭ𝔞𝔟𝔩𝔢𝔰.

The wrecks dissolve above us; their dust drops
    down from afar—
Down to the dark, to the utter dark, where the
    blind white sea-snakes are.
There is no sound, no echo of sound, in the des-
    erts of the deep,
Or the great gray level plains of ooze where the
    shell-burred cables creep.

Here in the womb of the world—here on the tie-
    ribs of earth
  Words, and the words of men, flicker and flut-
    ter and beat—
Warning, sorrow and gain, salutation and mirth—
  For a Power troubles the Still that has neither
    voice nor feet.

2

They have wakened the timeless Things ; they
have killed their father Time;
Joining hands in the gloom, a league from the
last of the sun.
Hush! Men talk to-day o'er the waste of the ulti-
mate slime,
And a new Word runs between: whispering,
"Let us be one!"

The Song of the Sons.

One from the ends of the earth—gifts at an open
door—
Treason has much, but we, Mother, thy sons have
more!
From the whine of a dying man, from the snarl of
a wolf-pack freed,
Turn, for the world is thine.   Mother, be proud of
thy seed!
Count, are we feeble or few ?   Hear, is our speech
so rude ?
Look, are we poor in the land ? Judge, are we
men of The Blood ?

Those that have stayed at thy knees, Mother, go
    call them in—
We that were bred overseas wait and would
    speak with our kin.
Not in the dark do we fight—haggle and flout and
    gibe;
Selling our love for a price, loaning our hearts for
    a bribe.
Gifts have we only to-day—Love without promise
    or fee—
Hear, for thy children speak, from the uttermost
    parts of the sea:

The Song of the Cities.

Bombay.

Royal and Dower-royal, I the Queen
    Fronting thy richest sea with richer hands—
A thousand mills roar through me where I glean
    All races from all lands.

Calcutta.

Me the Sea-captain loved, the River built,
    Wealth sought and Kings adventured life to hold.
Hail, England! I am Asia—Power on silt,
    Death in my hands, but Gold!

Madras.

Clive kissed me on the mouth and eyes and brow,
  Wonderful kisses, so that I became
Crowned above Queens—a withered beldame
      now,
  Brooding on ancient fame.

Rangoon.

Hail, Mother! Do they call me rich in trade?
  Little care I, but hear the shorn priest drone,
And watch my silk-clad lovers, man by maid,
  Laugh 'neath my Shwe Dagon.

Singapore.

Hail, Mother! East and West must seek my aid
  Ere the spent gear shall dare the ports afar.
The second doorway of the wide world's trade
  Is mine to loose or bar.

Hong-kong.

Hail, Mother! Hold me fast; my Praya sleeps
  Under innumerable keels to-day.
Yet guard (and landward) or to-morrow sweeps
  Thy warships down the bay.

Halifax.

Into the mist my guardian prows put forth,
  Behind the mist my virgin ramparts lie,
The Warden of the Honour of the North,
  Sleepless and veiled am I!

Quebec and Montreal.

Peace is our portion.   Yet a whisper rose,
  Foolish and causeless, half in jest, half hate.
Now wake we and remember mighty blows,
  And, fearing no man, wait!

Victoria.

From East to West the circling word has passed,
  Till West is East beside our land-locked blue;
From East to West the tested chain holds fast,
  The well-forged link rings true!

Capetown.

Hail! Snatched and bartered oft from hand to
    hand,
  I dream my dream, by rock and heath and pine,
Of Empire to the northward.   Ay, one land
  From Lion's Head to Line!

Melbourne.

Greeting! Nor fear nor favour won us place,
    Got between greed of gold and dread of drouth,
Loud-voiced and reckless as the wild tide-race
    That whips our harbour-mouth!

Sydney.

Greeting! My birth-stain have I turned to good;
    Forcing strong wills perverse to steadfastness;
The first flush of the tropics in my blood,
    And at my feet Success!

Brisbane.

The northern stirp* beneath the southern skies—
    I build a nation for an Empire's need,
Suffer a little, and my land shall rise,
    Queen over lands indeed!

Hobart.

Man's love first found me; man's hate made me
        Hell;
    For my babes' sake I cleansed those infamies.
Earnest for leave to live and labour well
    God flung me peace and ease.

* stock, race.

Auckland.

Last, loneliest, loveliest, exquisite, apart—
  On us, on us the unswerving season smiles,
Who wonder 'mid our fern why men depart
  To seek the Happy Isles!

England's Answer.

Truly ye come of The Blood; slower to bless than
    to ban;
Little used to lie down at the bidding of any man.
Flesh of the flesh that I bred, bone of the bone
    that I bare;
Stark as your sons shall be—stern as your fathers
    were.
Deeper than speech our love, stronger than life
    our tether,
But we do not fall on the neck nor kiss when we
    come together.
My arm is nothing weak, my strength is not gone
    by;
Sons, I have borne many sons but my dugs are
    not dry.

Look, I have made ye a place and opened wide
    the doors,

That ye may talk together, your Barons and Coun-
    cillors—

Wards of the Outer March, Lords of the Lower
    Seas,

Ay, talk to your gray mother that bore you on her
    knees!—

That ye may talk together, brother to brother's
    face—

Thus for the good of your peoples—thus for the
    Pride of the Race.

Also, we will make promise. So long as The
    Blood endures,

I shall know that your good is mine: ye shall feel
    that my strength is yours:

In the day of Armageddon, at the last great fight
    of all,

That Our House stand together and the pillars do
    not fall.

Draw now the three-fold knot firm on the nine-
    fold bands,

And the Law that ye make shall be law after the
    rule of your lands.

This for the waxen Heath, and that for the Wattle-
    bloom,

* Australian acacia.

This for the Maple-leaf, and that for the southern
    Broom.

The Law that ye make shall be law and I do not
    press my will,

Because ye are Sons of The Blood and call me
    Mother still.

Now must ye speak to your kinsmen and they
    must speak to you,

After the use of the English, in straight-flung words
    and few.

Go to your work and be strong, halting not in
    your ways,

Baulking the end half-won for an instant dole of
    praise.

Stand to your work and be wise—certain of sword
    and pen,

Who are neither children nor Gods, but men in a
    world of men!

THE FIRST CHANTEY. *(Matrosenlied)*

MINE was the woman to me, darkling I found
    her;
Haling her dumb from the camp, held her and
    bound her.
Hot rose her tribe on our track ere I had proved
    her;
Hearing her laugh in the gloom, greatly I loved
    her.

Swift through the forest we ran; none stood to
    guard us,
Few were my people and far; then the flood
    barred us—
Him we call Son of the Sea, sullen and swollen;
Panting we waited the death, stealer and stolen,

Yet ere they came to my lance laid for the
    slaughter,
Lightly she leaped to a log lapped in the water;

Holding on high and apart skins that arrayed her,
Called she the God of the Wind that he should aid
    her.

Life had the tree at that word, (Praise we the Giver!)
Otter-like left he the bank for the full river.
Far fell their axes behind, flashing and ringing,
Wonder was on me and fear, yet she was singing.

Low lay the land we had left. Now the blue
    bound us,
Even the Floor of the Gods level around us.
Whisper there was not, nor word, shadow nor
    showing,
Still the light stirred on the deep, glowing and
    growing.

Then did He leap to His place flaring from under,
He the Compeller, the Sun, bared to our wonder.
Nay, not a league from our eyes blinded with
    gazing,
Cleared He the womb of the world, huge and
    amazing!

This we beheld (and we live)—the Pit of the
    Burning,
Then the God spoke to the tree for our returning;

Back to the beach of our flight, fearless and slowly,
Back to our slayers he went: but we were holy.

Men that were hot in that hunt, women that
    followed,
Babes that were promised our bones, trembled
    and wallowed:
Over the necks of the tribe crouching and fawn-
    ing—
Prophet and priestess we came back from the
    dawning!

THE LAST CHANTEY.

"And there was no more sea."

THUS said The Lord in the Vault above the Cheru-
    bim,
Calling to the angels and the souls in their de-
  gree:
  "Lo! Earth has passed away
  On the smoke of Judgment Day.
That Our word may be established shall We
    gather up the sea?"

Loud sang the souls of the jolly, jolly mariners:
  "Plague upon the hurricane that made us furl
    and flee!
  But the war is done between us,
  In the deep the Lord hath seen us—
Our bones we'll leave the barracout', and God
    may sink the sea!"

21

Then said the soul of Judas that betrayèd Him:
> "Lord, hast Thou forgotten Thy covenant
> with me?
> How once a year I go
> To cool me on the floe,
> And Ye take my day of mercy if Ye take away
> the sea!"

Then said the soul of the Angel of the Off-shore
> Wind:
> (He that bits the thunder when the bull-mouthed
> breakers flee):
> "I have watch and ward to keep
> O'er Thy wonders on the deep,
> And Ye take mine honour from me if Ye take
> away the sea!"

Loud sang the souls of the jolly, jolly mariners:
> "Nay, but we were angry, and a hasty folk
> are we!
> If we worked the ship together
> Till she foundered in foul weather,
> Are we babes that we should clamour for a
> vengeance on the sea?"

Then said the souls of the slaves that men threw
overboard:
"Kennelled in the picaroon* a weary band
were we;
But Thy arm was strong to save,
And it touched us on the wave,
And we drowsed the long tides idle till Thy
Trumpets tore the sea."

Then cried the soul of the stout Apostle Paul to
God:
"Once we frapped a ship, and she laboured
woundily.
There were fourteen score of these,
And they blessed Thee on their knees,
When they learned Thy Grace and Glory under
Malta by the sea."

Loud sang the souls of the jolly, jolly mariners,
Plucking at their harps, and they plucked un-
handily:
"Our thumbs are rough and tarred,
And the tune is something hard—
May we lift a Deepsea Chantey such as seamen
use at sea?"

*and begird (to give strength)   2 dinali

Then said the souls of the gentlemen-adven-
    turers—
   Fettered wrist to bar all for red iniquity:
    "Ho, we revel in our chains
    O'er the sorrow that was Spain's;
   Heave or sink it, leave or drink it, we were
    masters of the sea!"

Up spake the soul of a gray Gothavn 'speck-
    shioner—
   (He that led the flinching in the fleets of fair
    Dundee):
    "Ho, the ringer and right whale,
    And the fish we struck for sale,
   Will Ye whelm them all for wantonness that
    wallow in the sea?"

Loud sang the souls of the jolly, jolly mariners,
   Crying: "Under Heaven, here is neither lead
    nor lea!
    Must we sing for evermore
    On the windless, glassy floor?
   Take back your golden fiddles and we'll beat to
    open sea!"

2 —*neer, one who cuts up speck (blubber)*
3 *sharpening*

Then stooped the Lord, and He called the good
sea up to Him,
And 'stablished his borders unto all eternity,
That such as have no pleasure
For to praise the Lord by measure,
They may enter into galleons and serve Him on
the sea.

Sun, wind, and cloud shall fail not from the face
of it,
Stinging, ringing spindrift, nor the fulmar flying
free;
And the ships shall go abroad
To the glory of the Lord
Who heard the silly sailor-folk and gave them
back their sea!

3
× mist for. wind driven spray
2 petrel.

THE MERCHANTMEN.

KING SOLOMON drew merchantmen,
  Because of his desire
For peacocks, apes, and ivory,
  From Tarshish unto Tyre:
With cedars out of Lebanon
  Which Hiram rafted down,
But we be only sailormen
  That use in London town.

*Coastwise—cross-seas—round the world and back
    again—*
  *Where the flaw shall head us or the full
      Trade suits—*
*Plain-sail—storm-sail—lay your board and tack
    again—*
  *And that's the way we'll pay Paddy Doyle for
      his boots!*

We bring no store of ingots,
  Of spice or precious stones,
But that we have we gathered
  With sweat and aching bones:

In flame beneath the tropics,
  In frost upon the floe,
And jeopardy of every wind
  That does between them go.

And some we got by purchase,
  And some we had by trade,
And some we found by courtesy
  Of pike and carronade,
At midnight, 'mid-sea meetings,
  For charity to keep,
And light the rolling homeward-bound
  That rode a foot too deep.

By sport of bitter weather
  We're walty, strained, and scarred
From the kentledge on the kelson
  To the slings upon the yard.
Six oceans had their will of us
  To carry all away—
Our galley 's in the Baltic,
  And our boom 's in Mossel Bay!

We've floundered off the Texel,
  Awash with sodden deals,
We've slipped from Valparaiso
  With the Norther at our heels:

+ short cannon   2 cranky, liable to roll.
3 pigs of iron for ballast. 4. a timber over keel.

We've ratched beyond the Crossets
    That tusk the Southern Pole,
And dipped our gunnels under
    To the dread Agulhas roll.

Beyond all outer charting
    We sailed where none have sailed,
And saw the land-lights burning
    On islands none have hailed;
Our hair stood up for wonder,
    But, when the night was done,
There danced the deep to windward
    Blue-empty 'neath the sun!

Strange consorts rode beside us
    And brought us evil luck;
The witch-fire climbed our channels,
    And danced on vane and truck:
Till, through the red tornado,
    That lashed us nigh to blind,
We saw The Dutchman plunging,
    Full canvas, head to wind!

We've heard the Midnight Leadsman
    That calls the black deep down—
Ay, thrice we've heard The Swimmer,
    The Thing that may not drown.

[handwritten: x laide to a fr. land   2 planks in loose rigging. 4 southernmost point of Africa]

On frozen bunt and gasket
  The sleet-cloud drave her hosts,
When, manned by more than signed with us,
  We passed the Isle o' Ghosts!

And north, amid the hummocks,
  A biscuit-toss below,
We met the silent shallop
  That frighted whalers know;
For, down a cruel ice-lane,
  That opened as he sped,
We saw dead Henry Hudson
  Steer, North by West, his dead.

So dealt God's waters with us
  Beneath the roaring skies,
So walked His signs and marvels
  All naked to our eyes:
But we were heading homeward
  With trade to lose or make—
Good Lord, they slipped behind us
  In the tailing of our wake!

Let go, let go the anchors;
  Now shamed at heart are we
To bring so poor a cargo home
  That had for gift the sea!

Let go the great bow-anchors—
    Ah, fools were we and blind—
The worst we baled with utter toil,
    The best we left behind!

Coastwise—cross-seas—round the world and back
    again,
    Whither the flaw shall fail us or the Trades
        drive down:
Plain-sail—storm-sail—lay your board and tack
    again—
    And all to bring a cargo up to London Town!

McANDREW'S HYMN.

LORD, Thou hast made this world below the shad-
    ow of a dream,
An', taught by time, I tak' it so—exceptin' always
    Steam.
From coupler-flange to spindle-guide I see Thy
    Hand, O God—
Predestination in the stride o' yon connectin'-rod.
John Calvin might ha' forged the same—enorr-
    mous, certain, slow—
Ay, wrought it in the furnace-flame—*my* "Insti-
    tutio."
I cannot get my sleep to-night; old bones are hard
    to please;
I'll stand the middle watch up here—alone wi'
    God an' these
My engines, after ninety days o' race an' rack an'
    strain
Through all the seas of all Thy world, slam-bang-
    in' home again.

Slam-bang too much—they knock a wee—the
    crosshead-gibs are loose;
But thirty thousand mile o' sea has gied them fair
    excuse. . . .
Fine, clear an' dark—a full-draught breeze, wi'
    Ushant out o' sight,
An' Ferguson relievin' Hay. Old girl, ye'll walk
    to-night!
His wife's at Plymouth. . . . Seventy—One—Two
    —Three since he began—
Three turns for Mistress Ferguson. . . . an' who's
    to blame the man?
There's none at any port for me, by drivin' fast or
    slow,
Since Elsie Campbell went to Thee, Lord, thirty
    years ago.
(The year the *Sarah Sands* was burned. Oh
    roads we used to tread,
Fra' Maryhill to Pollokshaws—fra' Govan to Park-
    head!)
Not but they're ceevil on the Board. Ye'll hear
    Sir Kenneth say:
"Good morrn, McAndrews! Back again? An'
    how's your bilge to-day?"
Miscallin' technicalities but handin' me my
    chair

To drink Madeira wi' three Earls—the auld Fleet
   Engineer,

That started as a boiler-whelp—when steam and
   he were low.

I mind the time we used to serve a broken pipe
   wi' tow.

Ten pound was all the pressure then—Eh! Eh!—
   a man wad drive;

An' here, our workin' gauges give one hunder'
   fifty-five!

We're creepin' on wi' each new rig—less weight
   an' larger power:

There'll be the loco-boiler next an' thirty knots an
   hour!

Thirty an' more.   What I ha' seen since ocean-
   steam began

Leaves me no doot for the machine: but what
   about the man?

The man that counts, wi' all his runs, one million
   mile o' sea:

Four time the span from earth to moon. . . . How
   far, O Lord, from Thee?

That wast beside him night an' day.   Ye mind
   my first typhoon?

It scoughed the skipper on his way to jock wi' the
   saloon.

I was not four and twenty then—Ye wadna judge
a child ?

I'd seen the Tropics first that run—new fruit, new
smells, new air—

How could I tell—blind-fou wi' sun—the Deil was
lurkin' there ?

By day like playhouse-scenes the shore slid past
our sleepy eyes;

By night those soft, lasceevious stars leered from
those velvet skies,

In port (we used no cargo-steam) I'd daunder
down the streets—

An ijjit grinnin' in a dream—for shells an' parra-
keets,

An' walkin'-sticks o' carved bamboo an' blowfish
stuffed an' dried—

Fillin' my bunk wi' rubbishry the Chief put overside.

Till, off Sumbawa Head, Ye mind, I heard a land-
breeze ca'

Milk-warm wi' breath o' spice an' bloom: "Mc-
Andrews, come awa'!"

Firm, clear an' low—no haste, no hate—the
ghostly whisper went,

Just statin' eevidential facts beyon' all argument:

Malay Arch.

"Your mither's God's a graspin' deil, the shadow
     o' yoursel',

"Got out o' books by meenisters clean daft on
     Heaven an' Hell.

"They mak' him in the Broomielaw, o' Glasgie
     cold an' dirt,

"A jealous, pridefu' fetich, lad, that's only strong
     to hurt,

"Ye'll not go back to Him again an' kiss His red-
     hot rod,

"But come wi' Us" (Now, who were *They?*)
     "an' know the Leevin' God,

"That does not kipper souls for sport or break a
     life in jest,

"But swells the ripenin' cocoanuts an' ripes the
     woman's breast."

An' there it stopped: cut off: no more; that quiet,
     certain voice—

For me, six months o' twenty-four, to leave or *(age)*
     take at choice.

'Twas on me like a thunderclap—it racked me
     through an' through—

Temptation past the show o' speech, unnamable
     an' new—

The Sin against the Holy Ghost? . . . An' under
     all, our screw.

✗ even fink m. salt & pepper.

That storm blew by but left behind her anchor-
shiftin' swell,

Thou knowest all my heart an' mind, Thou knowest, Lord, I fell.

Third on the *Mary Gloster* then, and first that
night in Hell!

Yet was Thy hand beneath my head: about my
feet Thy care—

Fra' Deli clear to Torres Strait, the trial o'
despair,

But when we touched the Barrier Reef Thy answer
to my prayer!

We dared na run that sea by night but lay an'
held our fire,

An' I was drowzin' on the hatch—sick—sick wi'
doubt an' tire:

*" Better the sight of eyes that see than wanderin'
o' desire ! "*

Ye mind that word? Clear as our gongs—again,
an' once again,

When rippin' down through coral-trash ran out
our moorin'-chain;

An' by Thy Grace I had the Light to see my duty
plain.

Light on the engine-room—no more—clear as our
carbons burn.

I've lost it since a thousand times, but never past
    return.

.   .   .   .   .   .

Obsairve!   Per annum we'll have here two thou-
    sand souls aboard—
Think not I dare to justify myself before the Lord,
But—average fifteen hunder' souls safe-borne fra
    port to port—
I *am* o' service to my kind.   Ye wadna' blame the
    thought?
Maybe they steam from grace to wrath—to sin by
    folly led,—
It isna mine to judge their path—their lives are on
    my head.
Mine at the last—when all is done it all comes
    back to me,
The fault that leaves six thousand ton a log upon
    the sea.
We'll tak' one stretch—three weeks an' odd by
    any road ye steer—
Fra' Cape Town east to Wellington—ye need an
    engineer.
Fail there—ye've time to weld your shaft—ay, eat
    it, ere ye're spoke,
Or make Kerguelen under sail — three jiggers
    burned wi' smoke!

An' home again, the Rio run: it's no child's play
to go

Steamin' to bell for fourteen days o' snow an' floe
an' blow—

The bergs like kelpies* overside that girn an' turn
an' shift

Whaur, grindin' like the Mills o' God, goes by the
big South drift.

(Hail, snow an' ice that praise the Lord: I've met
them at their work,

An' wished we had anither route or they anither
kirk.)

Yon's strain, hard strain, o' head an' hand, for
though Thy Power brings

All skill to naught, Ye'll understand a man must
think o' things.

Then, at the last, we'll get to port an' hoist their
baggage clear—

The passengers, wi' gloves an' canes—an' this is
what I'll hear:

"Well, thank ye for a pleasant voyage. The tender's comin' now."

While I go testin' follower-bolts an' watch the
skipper bow.

They've words for everyone but me—shake hands
wi' half the crew,

* horse shaped water-spirits (warning of death by drowning).
2 groin

Except the dour Scots engineer, the man they
  never knew.

An' yet I like the wark for all we've dam' few
  pickin's here—

No pension, an' the most we earn's four hunder'
  pound a year.

Better myself abroad? Maybe. *I'd* sooner starve
  than sail

Wi' such as call a snifter-rod *ross*. . . . French
  for nightingale.

Commeesion on my stores? Some do; but I can
  not afford

To lie like stewards wi' patty-pans. I'm older
  than the Board.

A bonus on the coal I save? Ou ay, the Scots are
  close,

But when I grudge the strength Ye gave I'll
  grudge their food to *those*.

(There's bricks that I might recommend—an' clink
  the fire-bars cruel.

No! Welsh—Wangarti at the worst—an' damn all
  patent fuel!)

Inventions? Ye must stay in port to mak' a
  patent pay.

My Deeferential Valve-Gear taught me how that
  business lay,

I blame no chaps wi' clearer head for aught they make or sell.

I found that I could not invent an' look to these—as well.

So, wrestled wi' Apollyon—Nah!—fretted like a bairn—

But burned the workin'-plans last run wi' all I hoped to earn.

Ye know how hard an Idol dies, an' what that meant to me—

E'en tak' it for a sacrifice acceptable to Thee. . . .

Below there! Oiler! What's your wark? Ye find her runnin' hard?

Ye needn't swill the cap wi' oil—this isn't the Cunard.

Ye thought? Ye are not paid to think. Go, sweat that off again!

Tck! Tck! It's deeficult to sweer nor tak' The Name in vain!

Men, ay an' women, call me stern. Wi' these to oversee

Ye'll note I've little time to burn on social repartee.

The bairns see what their elders miss; they'll hunt me to an' fro,

Till for the sake of—well, a kiss—I tak' 'em down below.

4

That minds me of our Viscount loon—Sir Ken-
neth's kin—the chap
Wi' russia leather tennis-shoon an' spar-decked*
yachtin'-cap.
I showed him round last week, o'er all—an' at the
last says he:
"Mister McAndrews, don't you think steam spoils
romance at sea?"
Damned ijjit! I'd been doon that morn to see
what ailed the throws,
Manholin', on my back—the cranks three inches
from my nose.
Romance! Those first-class passengers they like
it very well,
Printed an' bound in little books; but why don't
poets tell?
I'm sick of all their quirks an' turns—the loves an'
doves they dream—
Lord, send a man like Robbie Burns to sing the
Song o' Steam!
To match wi' Scotia's noblest speech yon orchestra
sublime
Whaurto—uplifted like the Just—the tail-rods mark
the time.
The crank-throws give the double-bass; the feed-
pump sobs an' heaves:

*upper deck. 2 movement of cranks.

An' now the main eccentrics start their quarrel on
the sheaves.

Her time, her own appointed time, the rocking
link-head bides,

Till—hear that note?—the rod's return whings
glimmerin' through the guides.

They're all awa! True beat, full power, the
clangin' chorus goes

Clear to the tunnel where they sit, my purrin'
dynamoes.

Interdependence absolute, foreseen, ordained, de-
creed,

To work, Ye'll note, at any tilt an' every rate o'
speed.

Fra skylight-lift to furnace-bars, backed, bolted,
braced an' stayed,

An' singin' like the Mornin' Stars for joy that they
are made;

While, out o' touch o' vanity, the sweatin' thrust-
block says:

"Not unto us the praise, or man—not unto us the
praise!"

Now, a' together, hear them lift their lesson—theirs
an' mine:

"Law, Orrder, Duty an' Restraint, Obedience, Dis-
cipline!"

Mill, forge an' try-pit taught them that when roar-
　　in' they arose,
An' whiles I wonder if a soul was gied them wi'
　　the blows.
Oh for a man to weld it then, in one trip-hammer
　　strain,
Till even first-class passengers could tell the mean-
　　in' plain!
But no one cares except mysel' that serve an' un-
　　derstand
My seven thousand horse-power here.　Eh, Lord!
　　They're grand—they're grand!
Uplift am I?　When first in store the new-made
　　beasties stood,
Were Ye cast down that breathed the Word de-
　　clarin' all things good?
Not so!　O' that warld-liftin' joy no after-fall
　　could vex,
Ye've left a glimmer still to cheer the Man—the
　　Arrtifex!
That holds, in spite o' knock and scale, o' friction,
　　waste an' slip,
An' by that light—now, mark my word—we'll
　　build the Perfect Ship.
I'll never last to judge her lines or take her curve—
　　not I.

But I ha' lived an' I ha' worked.   All thanks to
    Thee, Most High!

An' I ha' done what I ha' done—judge Thou if ill
    or well—

Always Thy Grace preventin' me. . . .

            Losh!   Yon's the "Stand by" bell.

Pilot so soon ?   His flare it is.   The mornin'-watch
    is set.

Well, God be thanked, as I was sayin', I'm no
    Pelagian yet.

Now I'll tak' on. . . .

   'Morrn, Ferguson.   Man, have ye ever thought

What your good leddy costs in coal ?   . . .   I'll
    burn 'em down to port.

THE MIRACLES.

I SENT a message to my dear—
  A thousand leagues and more to her—
The dumb sea-levels thrilled to hear,
  And Lost Atlantis bore to her.

Behind my message hard I came,
  And nigh had found a grave for me;
But that I launched of steel and flame
  Did war against the wave for me.

Uprose the deep, by gale on gale,
  To bid me change my mind again—
He broke his teeth along my rail,
  And, roaring, swung behind again.

I stayed the sun at noon to tell
  My way across the waste of it;
I read the storm before it fell
  And made the better haste of it.

46

Afar, I hailed the land at night—
    The towers I built had heard of me—
And, ere my rocket reached its height,
    Had flashed my Love the word of me.

Earth gave her chosen men of strength
    (They lived and strove and died for me)
To drive my road a nation's length,
    And toss the miles aside for me.

I snatched their toil to serve my needs—
    Too slow their fleetest flew for me—
I tired twenty smoking steeds,
    And bade them bait a new for me.

I sent the lightnings forth to see
    Where hour by hour she waited me.
Among ten million one was she,
    And surely all men hated me!

Dawn ran to meet us at my goal—
    Ah, day no tongue shall tell again!—
And little folk of little soul
    Rose up to buy and sell again!

THE NATIVE-BORN.

WE'VE drunk to the Queen—God bless her!—
    We've drunk to our mothers' land;
We've drunk to our English brother
    (But he does not understand);
We've drunk to the wide creation,
    And the Cross swings low to the morn,
Last toast, and of obligation,
    A health to the Native-born!

They change their skies above them,
    But not their hearts that roam!
We learned from our wistful mothers
    To call old England "home";
We read of the English sky-lark,
    Of the spring in the English lanes,
But we screamed with the painted lories
    As we rode on the dusty plains!

48

They passed with their old-world legends—
  Their tales of wrong and dearth—
Our fathers held by purchase,
  But we by the right of birth;
Our heart's where they rocked our cradle,
  Our love where we spent our toil,
And our faith and our hope and our honour
  We pledge to our native soil!

I charge you charge your glasses—
  I charge you drink with me
To the men of the Four New Nations,
  And the Islands of the Sea—
To the last least lump of coral
  That none may stand outside,
And our own good pride shall teach us
  To praise our comrade's pride.

To the hush of the breathless morning
  On the thin, tin, crackling roofs,
To the haze of the burned back-ranges
  And the dust of the shoeless hoofs—
To the risk of a death by drowning,
  To the risk of a death by drouth—
To the men of a million acres,
  To the Sons of the Golden South.

To the Sons of the Golden South, (Stand up!)
   And the life we live and know,
Let a fellow sing o' the little things he cares
      about,
If a fellow fights for the little things he cares
      about
   With the weight of a single blow!

To the smoke of a hundred coasters,
   To the sheep on a thousand hills,
To the sun that never blisters,
   To the rain that never chills—
To the land of the waiting springtime,
   To our five-meal, meat-fed men,
To the tall deep-bosomed women,
   And the children nine and ten!

And the children nine and ten, (Stand up!)
   And the life we live and know,
Let a fellow sing o' the little things he cares
      about,
If a fellow fights for the little things he cares
      about
   With the weight of a two-fold blow!

To the far-flung fenceless prairie
    Where the quick cloud-shadows trail,
To our neighbour's barn in the offing
    And the line of the new-cut rail;
To the plough in her league-long furrow
    With the gray Lake gulls behind—
To the weight of a half-year's winter
    And the warm wet western wind!

To the home of the floods and thunder,
    To her pale dry healing blue—
To the lift of the great Cape combers,
    And the smell of the baked Karroo.*
To the growl of the sluicing stamp-head—
    To the reef and the water-gold,
To the last and the largest Empire,
    To the map that is half unrolled!

To our dear dark foster-mothers,
    To the heathen songs they sung—
To the heathen speech we babbled
    Ere we came to the white man's tongue.
To the cool of our deep verandas—
    To the blaze of our jewelled main,
To the night, to the palms in the moonlight,
    And the fire-fly in the cane!

* dry plain in S. Africa

To the hearth of our people's people—
    To her well-ploughed windy sea,
To the hush of our dread high-altars
    Where the Abbey makes us We;
To the grist of the slow-ground ages,
    To the gain that is yours and mine—
To the Bank of the Open Credit,
    To the Power-house of the Line!

We've drunk to the Queen—God bless her!—
    We've drunk to our mothers' land;
We've drunk to our English brother
    (And we hope he'll understand).
We've drunk as much as we're able,
    And the Cross swings low to the morn;
Last toast—and your foot on the table!—
    A health to the Native-born!

A health to the Native-born, (Stand up!)
    We're six white men arow,
All bound to sing o' the little things we care
        about,
All bound to fight for the little things we care
        about
With the weight of a six-fold blow!
By the might of our cable-tow, (Take hands!)

From the Orkneys to the Horn,
  All round the world (*and a little loop to pull
      it by*),
All round the world (*and a little strap to buckle
      it*),
  A health to the Native-born !

THE KING.

"FAREWELL, Romance!" the Cave-men said;
 "With bone well carved he went away,
Flint arms the ignoble arrowhead,
 And jasper tips the spear to-day.
Changed are the Gods of Hunt and Dance,
And he with these.   Farewell, Romance!"

"Farewell, Romance!" the Lake-folk sighed;
 "We lift the weight of flatling years;
The caverns of the mountain side
 Hold him who scorns our hutted piers.
Lost hills whereby we dare not dwell,
Guard ye his rest.   Romance, farewell!"

"Farewell, Romance!" the Soldier spoke;
 "By sleight of sword we may not win,
But scuffle 'mid uncleanly smoke
 Of arquebus and culverin.
Honour is lost, and none may tell
Who paid good blows.   Romance, farewell!"

"Farewell, Romance!" the Traders cried;
   "Our keels ha' lain with every sea;
The dull-returning wind and tide
   Heave up the wharf where we would be;
The known and noted breezes swell
Our trudging sail.   Romance, farewell!"

"Good-bye, Romance!" the Skipper said;
   "He vanished with the coal we burn;
Our dial marks full steam ahead,
   Our speed is timed to half a turn.
Sure as the tidal trains we ply
'Twixt port and port.   Romance, good-bye!"

"Romance!" the Season-tickets mourn,
   "*He* never ran to catch his train,
But passed with coach and guard and horn—
   And left the local—late again!"
Confound Romance!" . . . And all unseen
Romance brought up the nine-fifteen.

His hand was on the lever laid,
   His oil-can soothed the worrying cranks,
His whistle waked the snowbound grade,
   His fog-horn cut the reeking Banks;
In dock and deep and mine and mill
The Boy-god reckless laboured still.

Robed, crowned and throned, he wove his
     spell,
     Where heart-blood beat or hearth-smoke
       curled,
With unconsidered miracle,
     Hedged in a backward-gazing world;
Then taught his chosen bard to say:
" The King was with us—yesterday ! "

THE RHYME OF THE THREE SEALERS.

Away by the lands of the Japanee,
*   When the paper lanterns glow*
And the crews of all the shipping drink
*   In the house of Blood Street Joe,*
At twilight, when the landward breeze
*   Brings up the harbour noise,*
And ebb of Yokohama Bay
*   Swigs* chattering through the buoys,*
In Cisco's Dewdrop Dining Rooms
*   They tell the tale anew*
Of a hidden sea and a hidden fight,
When the Baltic ran from the Northern Light
*   And the Stralsund fought the two!*

Now this is the Law of the Muscovite, that he
    proves with shot and steel,
When ye come by his isles in the Smoky Sea ye
    must not take the seal,
Where the gray sea goes nakedly between the
    weed-hung shelves,

smoke, draws.

And the little blue fox he is bred for his skin and
 the seal they breed for themselves;
For when the *matkas* seek the shore to drop their
 pups aland,
The great man-seal haul out of the sea, aroaring,
 band by band;
And when the first September gales have slaked
 their rutting-wrath,
The great man-seal haul back to the sea and no
 man knows their path.
Then dark they lie and stark they lie—rookery,
 dune, and floe,
And the Northern Lights come down o' nights to
 dance with the houseless snow.
And God who clears the grounding berg and steers
 the grinding floe,
He hears the cry of the little kit-fox and the lem-
 ming on the snow.
But since our women must walk gay and money
 buys their gear,
The sealing-boats they filch that way at hazard
 year by year.
English they be and Japanee that hang on the
 Brown Bear's flank,
And some be Scot, but the worst, God wot, and
 the boldest thieves, be Yank!

It was the sealer Northern Light, to the Smoky
    Seas she bore.

With a stovepipe stuck from a starboard port and
    the Russian flag at her fore.

(Baltic, Stralsund, and Northern Light—oh! they
    were birds of a feather—

Slipping away to the Smoky Seas, three seal-
    thieves together!)

And at last she came to a sandy cove and the Bal-
    tic lay therein,

But her men were up with the herding seal to
    drive and club and skin.

There were fifteen hundred skins abeach, cool pelt
    and proper fur,

When the Northern Light drove into the bight and
    the sea-mist drove with her.

The Baltic called her men and weighed—she could
    not choose but run—

For a stovepipe seen through the closing mist, it
    shows like a four-inch gun

(And loss it is that is sad as death to lose both trip
    and ship

And lie for a rotting contraband on Vladivostock
    slip).

She turned and dived in the sea-smother as a rab-
    bit dives in the whins,

& goose

And the Northern Light sent up her boats to steal
      the stolen skins.

They had not brought a load to side or slid their
      hatches clear,

When they were aware of a sloop-of-war, ghost-
      white and very near.

Her flag she showed, and her guns she showed—
      three of them, black, abeam,

And a funnel white with the crusted salt, but
      never a show of steam.

There was no time to man the brakes, they
      knocked the shackle free,

And the Northern Light stood out again, goose-
      winged to open sea.

(For life it is that is worse than death, by force of
      Russian law

To work in the mines of mercury that loose the
      teeth in your jaw!)

They had not run a mile from shore—they heard
      no shots behind—

When the skipper smote his hand on his thigh and
      threw her up in the wind:

"Bluffed—raised out on a bluff," said he, "for if
      my name's Tom Hall,

"You must set a thief to catch a thief—and a thief
    has caught us all!
"By every butt in Oregon and every spar in Maine,
"The hand that spilled the wind from her sail was
    the hand of Reuben Paine!
"He has rigged and trigged her with paint and
    spar, and, faith, he has faked her well—
"But I'd know the Stralsund's deckhouse yet from
    here to the booms o' Hell.
"Oh, once we ha' met at Baltimore, and twice on
    Boston pier,
"But the sickest day for you, Reuben Paine, was
    the day that you came here—
"The day that you came here, my lad, to scare us
    from our seal
"With your funnel made o' your painted cloth,
    and your guns o' rotten deal!
"Ring and blow for the Baltic now, and head her
    back to the bay,
"For we'll come into the game again with a
    double deck to play!"

They rang and blew the sealers' call—the poaching
    cry o' the sea—
And they raised the Baltic out of the mist, and an
    angry ship was she:

And blind they groped through the whirling
    white, and blind to the bay again,
Till they heard the creak of the Stralsund's boom
    and the clank of her mooring-chain.
They laid them down by bitt and boat, their pis-
    tols in their belts,
And: "Will you fight for it, Reuben Paine, or
    will you share the pelts?"

A dog-toothed laugh laughed Reuben Paine, and
    bared his flenching knife.
"Yea, skin for skin, and all that he hath a man
    will give for his life;
But I've six thousand skins below, and Yeddo
    Port to see,
And there's never a law of God or man runs north
    of Fifty-Three.
So go in peace to the naked seas with empty holds
    to fill,
And I'll be good to your seal this catch, as many as
    I shall kill."

'Answered the snap of a closing lock and the jar of
    a gun-butt slid,
But the tender fog shut fold on fold to hide the
    wrong they did.

timbers to hold cable.

The weeping fog rolled fold on fold the wrath of
man to cloak,

And the flame-spurts pale ran down the rail as
the sealing-rifles spoke.

The bullets bit on bend and butt,* the splinter sliv-
ered free,

(Little they trust to sparrow-dust that stop the
seal in his sea!)

The thick smoke hung and would not shift, leaden
it lay and blue,

But three were down on the Baltic's deck and two
of the Stralsund's crew.

An arm's length out and overside the banked fog
held them bound;

But, as they heard or groan or word, they fired at
the sound.

For one cried out on the name of God, and one to
have him cease;

And the questing volley found them both and
bade them hold their peace.

And one called out on a heathen joss and one on
the Virgin's Name;

And the schooling bullet leaped across and showed
them whence they came.

And in the waiting silences the rudder whined beneath,

*side o-end of planks.

And each man drew his watchful breath slow
    taken 'tween the teeth—
Trigger and ear and eye acock, knit brow and
    hard-drawn lips—
Bracing his feet by chock and cleat for the rolling
    of the ships:
Till they heard the cough of a wounded man that
    fought in the fog for breath,
Till they heard the torment of Reuben Paine that
    wailed upon his death:

"The tides they'll go through Fundy Race but I'll
    go never more
"And see the hogs from ebb-tide mark turn scam-
    pering back to shore.
"No more I'll see the trawlers drift below the Bass
    Rock ground,
"Or watch the tall Fall steamer lights tear blaz-
    ing up the Sound.
"Sorrow is me, in a lonely sea and a sinful fight I
    fall,
"But if there's law o' God or man you'll swing
    for it yet, Tom Hall!"

Tom Hall stood up by the quarter-rail. "Your
    words in your teeth," said he.

"There's never a law of God or man runs north
    of Fifty Three.

"So go in grace with Him to face, and an ill-
    spent life behind,

"And I'll take care o' your widows, Rube, as
    many as I shall find."

A Stralsund man shot blind and large, and a war-
    lock Finn was he,

And he hit Tom Hall with a bursting ball a hand's-
    breadth over the knee.

Tom Hall caught hold by the topping-lift, and sat
    him down with an oath,

"You'll wait a little, Rube," he said, "the Devil
    has called for both.

"The Devil is driving both this tide, and the kill-
    ing-grounds are close,

"And we'll go up to the Wrath of God as the
    holluschickie goes.

"O men, put back your guns again and lay
    your rifles by,

"We've fought our fight, and the best are down.
    Let up and let us die!

"Quit firing, by the bow there—quit! Call off
    the Baltic's crew!

"You're sure of Hell as me or Rube—but wait till
    we get through."

imfish 2. *tackle that holds up boom of mainsail*

There went no word between the ships, but thick
　　　and quick and loud
The life-blood drummed on the dripping decks,
　　　with the fog-dew from the shroud,
The sea-pull drew them side by side, gunnel to
　　　gunnel laid,
And they felt the sheerstrakes pound and clear,
　　　but never a word was said.

Then Reuben Paine cried out again before his
　　　spirit passed:
" Have I followed the sea for thirty years to die in
　　　the dark at last?
"Curse on her work that has nipped me here
　　　with a shifty trick unkind—
"I have gotten my death where I got my bread,
　　　but I dare not face it blind.
" Curse on the fog! Is there never a wind of all
　　　the winds I knew
" To clear the smother from off my chest, and let
　　　me look at the blue?"
The good fog heard—like a splitten sail, to left and
　　　right she tore,
And they saw the sun-dogs in the haze and the
　　　seal upon the shore.

*the flanders under gunwale.

Silver and gray ran spit and bay to meet the steel-
backed tide,
And pinched and white in the clearing light the
crews stared overside.
O rainbow-gay the red pools lay that swilled and
spilled and spread,
And gold, raw gold, the spent shell rolled between
the careless dead—
The dead that rocked so drunkenwise to weather
and to lee,
And they saw the work their hands had done as
God had bade them see!

And a little breeze blew over the rail that made
the headsails lift,
But no man stood by wheel or sheet, and they let
the schooners drift.
And the rattle rose in Reuben's throat and he cast
his soul with a cry,
And "Gone already?" Tom Hall he said.   "Then
it's time for me to die."
His eyes were heavy with great sleep and yearn-
ing for the land,
And he spoke as a man that talks in dreams, his
wound beneath his hand.

"Oh, there comes no good in the westering wind
    that backs against the sun;
"Wash down the decks—they're all too red—and
    share the skins and run,
"Baltic, Stralsund, and Northern Light,—clean
    share and share for all,
"You'll find the fleets off Tolstoi Mees, but you
    will not find Tom Hall.
"Evil he did in shoal-water and blacker sin on the
    deep,
"But now he's sick of watch and trick, and now
    he'll turn and sleep.
"He'll have no more of the crawling sea that
    made him suffer so,
"But he'll lie down on the killing-grounds where
    the holluschickie go.
"And west you'll turn and south again, beyond the
    sea-fog's rim,
"And tell the Yoshiwara girls to burn a stick for
    him.
"And you'll not weight him by the heels and
    dump him overside,
"But carry him up to the sand-hollows to die as
    Bering died,
"And make a place for Reuben Paine that knows
    the fight was fair,

"And leave the two that did the wrong to talk it
    over there!"

*Half-steam ahead by guess and lead, for the sun
    is mostly veiled—*
*Through fog to fog, by luck and log, sail ye as
    Bering sailed ;*
*And, if the light shall lift aright to give your land-
    fall plain,*
*North and by west, from Zapne Crest, ye raise
    the Crosses Twain.*
*Fair marks are they to the inner bay, the reckless
    poacher knows,*
*What time the scarred see-catchie lead their sleek
    seraglios.*
*Ever they hear the floe-pack clear, and the blast of
    the old bull-whale,*
*And the deep seal-roar that beats off shore above
    the loudest gale.*
*Ever they wait the winter's hate as the thundering
    boorga calls,*
*Where northward look they to St. George, and
    westward to St. Paul's.*
*Ever they greet the hunted fleet—lone keels off
    headlands drear—*

When the sealing-schooners flit that way at hazard
        year by year.
Ever in Yokohama Port men tell the tale anew
    Of a hidden sea and a hidden fight,
    When the Baltic ran from the Northern Light
And the Stralsund fought the two!

THE DERELICT.

" And reports the derelict *Mary Pollock* still at sea."

Shipping News.

I was the staunchest of our fleet
Till the Sea rose beneath our feet
Unheralded, in hatred past all measure.
Into his pits he stamped my crew,
Buffeted, blinded, bound and threw;
Bidding me eyeless wait upon his pleasure.

Man made me, and my will
Is to my maker still,
Whom now the currents con, the rollers steer—
Lifting forlorn to spy
Trailed smoke along the sky,
Falling afraid lest any keel come near.

Wrenched as the lips of thirst,
Wried, dried, and split and burst,
Bone-bleached my decks, wind-scoured to the
graining;

And, jarred at every roll,
The gear that was my soul
Answers the anguish of my beams' complaining.

For life that crammed me full,
Gangs of the prying gull
That shriek and scrabble on the riven hatches.
For roar that dumbed the gale
My hawse-pipes guttering wail,
Sobbing my heart out through the uncounted
watches.

Blind in the hot blue ring
Through all my points I swing—
Swing and return to shift the sun anew.
Blind in my well-known sky
I hear the stars go by,
Mocking the prow that can not hold one true!

White on my wasted path
Wave after wave in wrath
Frets 'gainst his fellow, warring where to send
me.
Flung forward, heaved aside,
Witless and dazed, I bide
The mercy of the comber that shall end me.

North where the bergs careen,
The spray of seas unseen
Smokes round my head and freezes in the fall-
ing;
South where the corals breed,
The footless, floating weed
Folds me and fouls me, strake on strake upcrawl-
ing.

I that was clean to run
My race against the sun—
Strength on the deep, am bawd to all disaster—
Whipped forth by night to meet
My sister's careless feet,
And with a kiss betray her to my master!

Man made me, and my will
Is to my maker still—
To him and his, our peoples at their pier:
Lifting in hope to spy
Trailed smoke along the sky;
Falling afraid lest any keel come near!

6

THE SONG OF THE BANJO.

You couldn't pack a Broadwood half a mile—
    You mustn't leave a fiddle in the damp—
You couldn't raft an organ up the Nile,
    And play it in an Equatorial swamp.
I travel with the cooking-pots and pails—
    *I'*m sandwiched 'tween the coffee and the
        pork—
And when the dusty column checks and tails,
    You should hear me spur the rearguard to a
        walk!

    With my " *Pilly-willy-winky-winky popp !* ''
        [O it's any tune that comes into my
          head!]
    So I keep 'em moving forward till they
          drop;
      So I play 'em up to water and to bed.

In the silence of the camp before the fight,
    When it's good to make your will and say
      your prayer,

You can hear my *strumpty-tumpty* overnight
   Explaining ten to one was always fair.
I'm the prophet of the Utterly Absurd,
   Of the Patently Impossible and Vain—
And when the Thing that Couldn't has occurred,
   Give me time to change my leg and go again.

   With my " *Tumpa - tumpa - tumpa - tum - pa
     tump !* "
     In the desert where the dung-fed camp-
     smoke curled
    There was never voice before us till I led
     our lonely chorus,
      I—the war-drum of the White Man round
      the world!

By the bitter road the Younger Son must tread,
   Ere he win to hearth and saddle of his own,—
'Mid the riot of the shearers at the shed,
   In the silence of the herder's hut alone—
In the twilight, on a bucket upside down,
   Hear me babble what the weakest won't con-
   fess—
I am Memory and Torment—I am Town!
   I am all that ever went with evening dress!

With my " *Tunk-a   tunka-tunka-tunka-*
        tunk ! "
[So the lights—the London lights—grow
        near and plain!]
So I rowel 'em afresh towards the Devil and
        the Flesh,
    Till I bring my broken rankers home again.

In desire of many marvels over sea,
    Where the new-raised tropic city sweats and
        roars,
I have sailed with Young Ulysses from the quay
    Till the anchor rumbled down on stranger
        shores.
He is blooded to the open and the sky,
    He is taken in a snare that shall not fail,
He shall hear me singing strongly, till he die,
    Like the shouting of a backstay in a gale.

With my " *Hya ! Heeya ! Heeya ! Hullah !*
        Haul ! "
[O the green that thunders aft along the
        deck!]
Are you sick o' towns and men ? You
        must sign and sail again,
    For it's "Johnny Bowlegs, pack your kit
        and trek!"

blooded to blood (of a hound)

Through the gorge that gives the stars at noon-
day clear—
    Up the pass that packs the scud beneath our
wheel—
Round the bluff that sinks her thousand fathom
sheer—
    Down the valley with our guttering brakes
asqueal:
Where the trestle groans and quivers in the
snow,
    Where the many-shedded levels loop and
twine,
So I lead my reckless children from below
    Till we sing the Song of Roland to the pine.

    With my " *Tinka-tinka-tinka-tinka-tink!* "
        [And the axe has cleared the mountain,
croup and crest!]
    So we ride the iron stallions down to drink,
        Through the cañons to the waters of the
West!

And the tunes that mean so much to you
alone—
    Common tunes that make you choke and
blow your nose,

Vulgar tunes that bring the laugh that brings the
groan—
I can rip your very heartstrings out with
those;
With the feasting, and the folly, and the fun—
And the lying, and the lusting, and the drink,
And the merry play that drops you, when
you're done,
To the thoughts that burn like irons if you
think.

With my " *Plunka - lunka - lunka - lunka-
lunk !* "
Here's a trifle on account of pleasure past,
Ere the wit that made you win gives you
eyes to see your sin
And the heavier repentance at the last.

Let the organ moan her sorrow to the roof—
I have told the naked stars the grief of man.
Let the trumpets snare the foeman to the proof—
I have known Defeat, and mocked it as we ran.
My bray ye may not alter nor mistake
When I stand to jeer the fatted Soul of Things,
But the Song of Lost Endeavour that I make,
Is it hidden in the twanging of the strings ?

With my " *Ta-ra-rara-rara-ra-ra-rrrp!* "
    [Is it naught to you that hear and pass
      me by?]
But the word—the word is mine, when the
    order moves the line
    And the lean, locked ranks go roaring
      down to die.

The grandam of my grandam was the Lyre—
    [O the blue below the little fisher-huts!]
That the Stealer stooping beachward filled with
    fire,
    Till she bore my iron head and ringing guts!
By the wisdom of the centuries I speak—
    To the tune of yestermorn I set the truth—
I, the joy of life unquestioned—I, the Greek—
    I, the everlasting Wonder Song of Youth!

    With my " *Tinka-tinka-tinka-tinka-tink!* "
      [What d'ye lack, my noble masters?
      What d'ye lack?]
    So I draw the world together link by link:
      Yea, from Delos up to Limerick and
      back!

"THE LINER SHE'S A LADY."

THE Liner she's a lady, 'an she never looks nor
    'eeds—
The Man-o'-War's 'er 'usband, an' 'e gives 'er all
    she needs;
But, oh, the little cargo-boats, that sail the wet
    seas roun',
They're just the same as you an' me a-plyin' up
    an' down!

Plyin' up an' down, Jenny, 'angin' round the
    Yard,
All the way by Fratton tram down to Ports-
    mouth 'Ard ;
Anythin' for business, an' we're growin' old—
Plyin' up an' down, Jenny, waitin' in the
    cold !

The Liner she's a lady by the paint upon 'er face,
An' if she meets an accident they call it sore dis-
    grace:

The Man-o'-War's 'er 'usband, and 'e's always
'andy by,
But, oh, the little cargo-boats! they've got to load
or die.

The Liner she's a lady, and 'er route is cut an'
dried;
The Man-o'-War's 'er 'usband, an' 'e always keeps
beside;
But, oh, the little cargo-boats that 'aven't any
man!
They've got to do their business first, and make
the most they can.

The Liner she's a lady, and if a war should
come,
The Man-o'-War's 'er 'usband, and 'e'd bid 'er stay
at home;
But, oh, the little cargo-boats that fill with every
tide!
'E'd 'ave to up an' fight for them, for they are
England's pride.

The Liner she's a lady, but if she wasn't made,
There still would be the cargo-boats for 'ome an'
foreign trade.

The Man-o'-War's 'er 'usband, but if we wasn't
    'ere,
'E wouldn't have to fight at all for 'ome an' friends
    so dear.

'Ome an' friends so dear, Jenny, 'angin' round
    the Yard,
All the way by Fratton tram down to Ports-
    mouth 'Ard;
Anythin' for business, an' we're growin' old—
'Ome an' friends so dear, Jenny, waitin' in the
    cold!

MULHOLLAND'S CONTRACT.

The fear was on the cattle, for the gale was on the
    sea,
An' the pens broke up on the lower deck an' let
    the creatures free—
An' the lights went out on the lower deck, an' no
    one down but me.

I had been singin' to them to keep 'em quiet
    there,
For the lower deck is the dangerousest, requirin'
    constant care,
An' give to me as the strongest man, though used
    to drink and swear.

I see my chance was certain of bein' horned or
    trod,
For the lower deck was packed with steers thicker
    'n peas in a pod,
An' more pens broke at every roll—so I made a
    Contract with God.

An' by the terms of the Contract, as I have read
    the same,
If He got me to port alive I would exalt His
    name,
An' praise His Holy Majesty till further orders
    came.

He saved me from the cattle an' He saved me from
    the sea,
For they found me 'tween two drownded ones
    where the roll had landed me—
An' a four-inch crack on top of my head, as crazy
    as could be.

But that were done by a stanchion, an' not by a
    bullock at all,
An' I lay still for seven weeks convalessing of the
    fall,
An' readin' the shiny Scripture texts in the Sea-
    men's Hospital.

An' I spoke to God of our Contract, an' He says
    to my prayer:
" I never puts on My ministers no more than they
    can bear.
" So back you go to the cattle-boats an' preach
    My Gospel there.

"For human life is chancy at any kind of trade,
"But most of all, as well you know, when the
steers are mad-afraid;
"So you go back to the cattle-boats an' preach
'em as I've said.

"They must quit drinkin' an' swearin', they
mustn't knife on a blow,
"They must quit gamblin' their wages, and you
must preach it so;
"For now those boats are more like Hell than
anything else I know."

I didn't want to do it, for I knew what I should
get,
An' I wanted to preach Religion, handsome an'
out of the wet,
But the Word of the Lord were lain on me, an' I
done what I was set.

I have been smit an' bruisèd, as warned would be
the case,
An' turned my cheek to the smiter exactly as Scripture says;
But following that, I knocked him down an' led
him up to Grace.

An' we have preaching on Sundays whenever the
    sea is calm,
An' I use no knife nor pistol an' I never take no
    harm,
For the Lord abideth back of me to guide my
    fighting arm.

An' I sign for four pound ten a month and save the
    money clear,
An' I am in charge of the lower deck, an' I never
    lose a steer;
An' I believe in. Almighty God an' I preach His
    Gospel here.

The skippers say I'm crazy, but I can prove 'em
    wrong,
For I am in charge of the lower deck with all that
    doth belong—
*Which they would not give to a lunatic, and the
    competition so strong!*

ANCHOR SONG.

(From Many Inventions).

HEH! Walk her round.   Heave, ah heave her short
    again!
  Over, snatch her over, there, and hold her on
    the pawl.
Loose all sail, and brace your yards aback and
    full—
  Ready jib to pay her off and heave short all!

  Well, ah fare you well; we can stay no more
    with you, my love—
    Down, set down your liquor and your girl
      from off your knee;
        For the wind has come to say:
        " You must take me while you may,
      If you'd go to Mother Carey,
      (Walk her down to Mother Carey!)
    Oh, we're bound to Mother Carey where
    she feeds her chicks at sea!"

✗ ratchet on capstan.

Heh! Walk her round.   Break, ah break it out o'
    that!
  Break our starboard bower out, apeak, awash,
    and clear.
Port—port she casts, with the harbour-roil beneath
    her foot,
  And that's the last o' bottom we shall see this
    year!

  Well, ah fare you well, for we've got to take
    her out again—
    Take her out in ballast, riding light and
    cargo-free.
        And it's time to clear and quit
        When the hawser grips the bitt,
    So we'll pay you with the foresheet and a
    promise from the sea!

Heh! Tally on!   Aft and walk away with her!
  Handsome to the cathead, now; O tally on the
    fall!
Stop, seize and fish, and easy on the davit-guy.
  Up, well up the fluke of her, and inboard haul!

  Well, ah fare you well, for the Channel wind's
    took hold of us,

Choking down our voices as we snatch the
gaskets free.
And it's blowing up for night,
And she's dropping Light on Light,
And she's snorting under bonnets for a
breath of open sea.

Wheel, full and by; but she'll smell her road alone
to-night.
Sick she is and harbour-sick—O sick to clear the
land!
Roll down to Brest with the old Red Ensign
over us—
Carry on and thrash her out with all she'll
stand!

Well, ah fare you well, and it's Ushant gives
the door to us,
Whirling like a windmill on the dirty scud
to lea:
Till the last, last flicker goes
From the tumbling water-rows,
And we're off to Mother Carey
(Walk her down to Mother Carey!)
Oh, we're bound for Mother Carey where
she feeds her chicks at sea!
7

THE SEA-WIFE.

THERE dwells a wife by the Northern Gate,
 And a wealthy wife is she;
She breeds a breed o' rovin' men
 And casts them over sea,

And some are drowned in deep water,
 And some in sight o' shore,
And word goes back to the weary wife,
 And ever she sends more.

For since that wife had gate and gear,
 And hearth and garth and bield,
She willed her sons to the white harvest,
 And that is a bitter yield.

She wills her sons to the wet ploughing,
 To ride the horse of tree;
And syne her sons come home again
 Far-spent from out the sea.

The good wife's sons come home again
   With little into their hands,
But the lore of men that ha' dealt with men
   In the new and naked lands.

But the faith of men that ha' brothered men
   By more than the easy breath,
And the eyes o' men that ha' read wi' men
   In the open books of death.

Rich are they, rich in wonders seen,
   But poor in the goods o' men,
So what they ha' got by the skin o' their teeth
   They sell for their teeth again.

For whether they lose to the naked skin,
   Or win to their hearts' desire,
They tell it all to the weary wife
   That nods beside the fire.

Her hearth is wide to every wind
   That makes the white ash spin;
And tide and tide and 'tween the tides
   Her sons go out and in;

(Out with great mirth that do desire
　　Hazard of trackless ways,
In with content to wait their watch
　　And warm before the blaze);

And some return by failing light,
　　And some in waking dream,
For she hears the heels of the dripping ghosts
　　That ride the rough roof-beam.

Home, they come home from all the ports,
　　The living and the dead;
The good wife's sons come home again
　　For her blessing on their head!

HYMN BEFORE ACTION.

THE earth is full of anger,
    The seas are dark with wrath;
The Nations in their harness
    Go up against our path!
Ere yet we loose the legions—
    Ere yet we draw the blade,
Jehovah of the Thunders,
    Lord God of Battles, aid!

High lust and froward bearing,
    Proud heart, rebellious brow—
Deaf ear and soul uncaring,
    We seek Thy mercy now:
The sinner that forswore Thee,
    The fool that passed Thee by,
Our times are known before Thee—
    Lord, grant us strength to die!

For those who kneel beside us
    At altars not Thine own,
Who lack the lights that guide us,
    Lord, let their faith atone;
If wrong we did to call them,
    By honour bound they came;
Let not Thy wrath befall them,
    But deal to us the blame.

From panic, pride, and terror,
    Revenge that knows no rein—
Light haste and lawless error,
    Protect us yet again.
Cloak Thou our undeserving,
    Make firm the shuddering breath,
In silence and unswerving
    To taste thy lesser death!

Ah, Mary pierced with sorrow,
    Remember, reach and save
The soul that comes to-morrow
    Before the God that gave!
Since each was born of woman,
    For each at utter need—
True comrade and true foeman,
    Madonna, intercede!

E'en now their vanguard gathers,
    E'en now we face the fray—
As Thou didst help our fathers,
    Help Thou our host to-day!
Fulfilled of signs and wonders,
    In life, in death made clear—
Jehovah of the Thunders,
    Lord God of Battles, hear!

TO THE TRUE ROMANCE.

(From Many Inventions.)

Thy face is far from this our war,
Our call and counter-cry,
I shall not find Thee quick and kind,
Nor know Thee till I die:
Enough for me in dreams to see
And touch Thy garments' hem:
Thy feet have trod so near to God
I may not follow them.

Through wantonness if men profess
  They weary of Thy parts,
E'en let them die at blasphemy
  And perish with their arts;
But we that love, but we that prove
  Thine excellence august,
While we adore discover more
  Thee perfect, wise, and just.

Since spoken word Man's Spirit stirred
  Beyond his belly-need,
What is is Thine of fair design
  In thought and craft and deed;

Each stroke aright of toil and fight,
  That was and that shall be,
And hope too high, wherefore we die,
  Has birth and worth in Thee.

Who holds by Thee hath Heaven in fee
  To gild his dross thereby,
And knowledge sure that he endure
  A child until he die—
For to make plain that man's disdain
  Is but new Beauty's birth—
For to possess, in loneliness,
  The joy of all the earth.

As Thou didst teach all lovers speech,
  And Life all mystery,
So shalt Thou rule by every school
  Till love and longing die,
Who wast or yet the lights were set,
  A whisper in the Void,
Who shalt be sung through planets young
  When this is clean destroyed.

Beyond the bounds our staring rounds,
  Across the pressing dark,
The children wise of outer skies
  Look hitherward and mark

A light that shifts, a glare that drifts,
    Rekindling thus and thus,
Not all forlorn, for Thou hast borne
    Strange tales to them of us.

Time hath no tide but must abide
    The servant of Thy will;
Tide hath no time, for to Thy rhyme
    The ranging stars stand still—
Regent of spheres that lock our fears
    Our hopes invisible,
Oh 'twas certes at Thy decrees
    We fashioned Heaven and Hell!

Pure Wisdom hath no certain path
    That lacks thy morning-eyne,
And captains bold by Thee controlled
    Most like to Gods design;
Thou art the Voice to kingly boys
    To lift them through the fight,
And Comfortress of Unsuccess,
    To give the dead good-night—

A veil to draw 'twixt God His Law
    And Man's infirmity,
A shadow kind to dumb and blind
    The shambles where we die;

A sum to trick th' arithmetic
    Too base of leaguing odds,
The spur of trust, the curb of lust,
    Thou handmaid of the Gods!

Oh Charity, all patiently
    Abiding wrack and scaith!
Oh Faith, that meets ten thousand cheats
    Yet drops no jot of faith!
Devil and brute Thou dost transmute
    To higher, lordlier show,
Who art in sooth that lovely Truth
    The careless angels know!

Thy face is far from this our war,
    Our call and counter-cry,
I may not find Thee quick and kind,
    Nor meet Thee till I die.

Yet may I look with heart unshook
    On blow brought home or missed—
Yet may I hear with equal ear
    The clarions down the list;
Yet set my lance above mischance
    And ride the barriere—
Oh, hit or miss, how little 'tis,
    My Lady is not there!

THE FLOWERS.

"To our private taste, there is always something a little exotic, almost artificial, in songs which, under an English aspect and dress, are yet so manifestly the product of other skies. They affect us like translations; the very fauna and flora are alien, remote; the dog's-tooth violet is but an ill substitute for the rathe primrose, nor can we ever believe that the wood-robin sings as sweetly in April as the English thrush."—*The Athenæum.*

Buy my English posies—
    Kent and Surrey may,
Violets of the Undercliff
    Wet with Channel spray;
Cowslips from a Devon combe
    Midland furze afire—
Buy my English posies,
    And I'll sell your hearts' desire!

Buy my English posies!—
    You that scorn the may
Won't you greet a friend from home
    Half the world away?

100

+ = coomb, hollow dale.

Green against the draggled drift,
    Faint and frail and first—
Buy my Northern blood-root
    And I'll know where you were nursed!
Robin down the logging-road whistles, "Come
    to me,"
Spring has found the maple-grove, the sap is run-
    ning free;
All the winds o' Canada call the ploughing-
    rain.
Take the flower and turn the hour, and kiss your
    love again!

Buy my English posies!—
    Here's to match your need.
Buy a tuft of royal heath,
    Buy a bunch of weed
White as sand of Muysenberg
    Spun before the gale—
Buy my heath and lilies
    And I'll tell you whence you hail!
Under hot Constantia broad the vineyards
    lie—
Throned and thorned the aching berg props the
    speckless sky—

Slow below the Wynberg firs trails the tilted
　　　wain—
Take the flower and turn the hour, and kiss your
　　　love again!

　　　Buy my English posies!—
　　　　You that will not turn,
　　　Buy my hot-wood clematis,
　　　　Buy a frond o' fern
　　　Gathered where the Erskine leaps
　　　　Down the road to Lorne—
　　　Buy my Christmas creeper
　　　　And I'll say where you were born!
West away from Melbourne dust holidays begin—
They that mock at Paradise woo at Cora Lynn—
Through the great South Otway gums sings the
　　　great South Main—
Take the flower and turn the hour, and kiss your
　　　love again!

　　　Buy my English posies!—
　　　　Here's your choice unsold!
　　　Buy a blood-red myrtle-bloom,
　　　　Buy the kowhai's gold

Flung for gift on Taupo's face
  Sign that spring is come—
Buy my clinging myrtle
  And I'll give you back your home!
Broom behind the windy town ; pollen o' the
    pine—
Bell-bird in the leafy deep where the *ratas*
    twine—
Fern above the saddle-bow, flax upon the plain—
Take the flower and turn the hour, and kiss your
    love again!

Buy my English posies!
  Ye that have your own
Buy them for a brother's sake
  Overseas, alone.
Weed ye trample underfoot
  Floods his heart abrim—
Bird ye never heeded,
  Oh, she calls his dead to him!
Far and far our homes are set round the Seven Seas.
Woe for us if we forget, we that hold by these!
Unto each his mother-beach, bloom and bird and
    land—
Masters of the Seven Seas, oh, love and under-
    stand!

THE LAST RHYME OF TRUE THOMAS.

The King has called for priest and cup,
  The King has taken spur and blade
To dub True Thomas a belted knight,
  And all for the sake o' the songs he made.

They have sought him high, they have sought
    him low,
  They have sought him over down and lea;
They have found him by the milk-white thorn
  That guards the gates o' Faerie.

'Twas bent beneath and blue above,
  Their eyes were held that they might not see
The kine that grazed between the knowes,
  Oh, they were the Queens o' Faerie!

"Now cease your song," the King he said,
  "Oh, cease your song and get you dight
To vow your vow and watch your arms,
  For I will dub you a belted knight.

104

coarse grass.   2 knoll.

"For I will give you a horse o' pride,
　Wi' blazon and spur and page and squire;
Wi' keep and tail and seizin and law,
　And land to hold at your desire."

True Thomas smiled above his harp,
　And turned his face to the naked sky,
Where, blown before the wastrel wind,
　The thistle-down she floated by.

"I ha' vowed my vow in another place,
　And bitter oath it was on me,
I ha' watched my arms the lee-long night,
　Where five-score fighting-men would flee.

"My lance is tipped o' the hammered flame,
　My shield is beat o' the moonlight cold;
And I won my spurs in the Middle World,
　A thousand fathoms beneath the mould.

"And what should I make wi' a horse o' pride,
　And what should I make wi' a sword so brown,
But spill the rings o' the Gentle Folk
　And flyte my kin in the Fairy Town?
8

"And what should I make wi' blazon and belt,
    Wi' keep and tail and seizin and fee,
And what should I do wi' page and squire
    That am a king in my own countrie?

"For I send east and I send west,
    And I send far as my will may flee,
By dawn and dusk and the drinking rain,
    And syne my Sendings return to me.

"They come wi' news of the groanin' earth,
    They come wi' news o' the roarin' sea,
Wi' word of Spirit and Ghost and Flesh,
    And man that's mazed among the three."

The King he bit his nether lip,
    And smote his hand upon his knee:
"By the faith o' my soul, True Thomas," he said,
    "Ye waste no wit in courtesie!

"As I desire, unto my pride,
    Can I make Earls by three and three,
To run before and ride behind
    And serve the sons o' my body."

" And what care I for your row-foot earls,
  Or all the sons o' your body ?
Before they win to the Pride o' Name,
  I trow they all ask leave o' me.

" For I make Honour wi' muckle mouth,
  As I make Shame wi' mincin' feet,
To sing wi' the priests at the market-cross,
  Or run wi' the dogs in the naked street.

" And some they give me the good red gold,
  And some they give me the white money,
And some they give me a clout o' meal,
  For they be people o' low degree.

" And the song I sing for the counted gold
  The same I sing for the white money,
But best I sing for the clout o' meal
  That simple people given me."

The King cast down a silver groat,
  A silver groat o' Scots money,
" If I come with a poor man's dole," he said,
  " True Thomas, will ye harp to me ? "

"Whenas I harp to the children small,
    They press me close on either hand:
And who are you," True Thomas said,
    "That you should ride while they must stand?

"Light down, light down from your horse o' pride,
    I trow ye talk too loud and hie,
And I will make you a triple word,
    And syne, if ye dare, ye shall 'noble me."

He has lighted down from his horse o' pride,
    And set his back against the stone.
"Now guard you well," True Thomas said,
    "Ere I rax your heart from your breast-bone!

True Thomas played upon his harp,
    The fairy harp that couldna' lee,
And the first least word the proud King heard,
    It harpit the salt tear out o' his ee.

"Oh, I see the love that I lost long syne,
    I touch the hope that I may not see,
And all that I did o' hidden shame,
    Like little snakes they hiss at me.

"The sun is lost at noon—at noon!
  The dread o' doom has grippit me.
True Thomas, hide me under your cloak,
  God wot, I'm little fit to dee!"

'Twas bent beneath and blue above—
  'Twas open field and running flood—
Where, hot on heath and dyke and wall,
  The high sun warmed the adder's brood.

"Lie down, lie down," True Thomas said.
  "The God shall judge when all is done;
But I will bring you a better word
  And lift the cloud that I laid on."

True Thomas played upon his harp,
  That birled and brattled to his hand,
And the next least word True Thomas made,
  It garred the King take horse and brand.

"Oh, I hear the tread o' the fighting-men,
  I see the sun on splent and spear!
I mark the arrow outen the fern!
  That flies so low and sings so clear!

x made. 2 armor plate. 2 birl, rattle

"Advance my standards to that war,
    And bid my good knights prick and ride;
The gled shall watch as fierce a fight
    As e'er was fought on the Border side!"

*'Twas bent beneath and blue above,
    'Twas nodding grass and naked sky,
Where ringing up the wastrel wind
    The eyass stooped upon the pye.*

True Thomas sighed above his harp,
    And turned the song on the midmost string;
And the last least word True Thomas made
    He harpit his dead youth back to the King.

"Now I am prince, and I do well
    To love my love withouten fear;
To walk wi' man in fellowship,
    And breathe my horse behind the deer.

"My hounds they bay unto the death,
    The buck has couched beyond the burn,
My love she waits at her window
    To wash my hands when I return.

kite 2 young hawk 3 magpie

"For that I live am I content
　　(Oh! I have seen my true love's eyes!)
To stand wi' Adam in Eden-glade,
　　And run in the woods o' Paradise!"

'Twas nodding grass and naked sky,
　'Twas blue above and bent below,
Where, checked against the wastrel wind,
　The red deer belled to call the doe.

True Thomas laid his harp away,
　　And louted low at the saddle-side;
He has taken stirrup and hauden rein,
　　And set the King on his horse o' pride.

"Sleep ye or wake," True Thomas said,
　"That sit so still, that muse so long;
Sleep ye or wake?—till the latter sleep
　　I trow ye'll not forget my song.

"I ha' harpit a shadow out o' the sun
　　To stand before your face and cry;
I ha' armed the earth beneath your heel,
　　And over your head I ha' dusked the sky!

"I ha' harpit ye up to the Throne o' God,
    I ha' harpit your secret soul in three;
I ha' harpit ye down to the Hinges o' Hell,
    And—ye—would—make—a Knight o' me!"

THE STORY OF UNG.

Once, on a glittering ice-field, ages and ages
    ago,
Ung, a maker of pictures, fashioned an image of
    snow.
Fashioned the form of a tribesman — gaily he
    whistled and sung,
Working the snow with his fingers. *Read ye the
    Story of Ung!*

Pleased was his tribe with that image—came in
    their hundreds to scan—
Handled it, smelt it, and grunted: "Verily, this is
    a man!
Thus do we carry our lances—thus is a war-belt
    slung.
Ay, it is even as we are. Glory and honour to
    Ung!"

Later he pictured an aurochs—later he pictured a
     bear—
Pictured the sabre-tooth tiger dragging a man to
     his lair—
Pictured the mountainous mammoth, hairy, ab-
     horrent, alone—
Out of the love that he bore them, scribing them
     clearly on bone.

Swift came the tribe to behold them, peering and
     pushing and still—
Men of the berg-battered beaches, men of the
     boulder-hatched hill,
Hunters and fishers and trappers—presently whis-
     pering low;
" Yea, they are like—and it may be . . . . But how
     does the Picture-man know ?

" Ung—hath he slept with the Aurochs—watched
     where the Mastodon roam ?
Spoke on the ice with the Bow-head—followed
     the Sabre-tooth home ?
Nay !   These are toys of his fancy !   If he have
     cheated us so,
How is there truth in his image—the man that he
     fashioned of snow ? "

Wroth was that maker of pictures—hotly he an-
    swered the call:
"Hunters and fishers and trappers, children and
    fools are ye all!
Look at the beasts when ye hunt them!" Swift
    from the tumult he broke,
Ran to the cave of his father and told him the
    shame that they spoke.

And the father of Ung gave answer, that was old
    and wise in the craft,
Maker of pictures aforetime, he leaned on his lance
    and laughed:
"If they could see as thou seest they would do
    what thou hast done,
And each man would make him a picture, and—
    what would become of my son?

"There would be no pelts of the reindeer, flung
    down at thy cave for a gift,
Nor dole of the oily timber that strands with the
    Baltic drift;
No store of well-drilled needles, nor ouches of
    amber pale;
No new-cut tongues of the bison, nor meat of the
    stranded whale.

" *Thou* hast not toiled at the fishing when the sodden trammels* freeze,

Nor worked the war-boats outward, through the
rush of the rock-staked seas,

Yet they bring thee fish and plunder—full meal
and an easy bed—

And all for the sake of thy pictures." And Ung
held down his head.

" *Thou* hast not stood to the aurochs when the
red snow reeks of the fight;

Men have no time at the houghing to count his
curls aright:

And the heart of the hairy mammoth thou sayest
they do not see,

Yet they save it whole from the beaches and broil
the best for thee.

"And now do they press to thy pictures, with
open mouth and eye,

And a little gift in the doorway, and the praise no
gift can buy:

But—sure they have doubted thy pictures, and
that is a grievous stain—

Son that can see so clearly, return them their gifts
again."

* long net.

And Ung looked down at his deerskins — their
    broad shell-tasselled bands—
And Ung drew downward his mitten and looked
    at his naked hands;
And he gloved himself and departed, and he heard
    his father, behind:
"Son that can see so clearly, rejoice that thy tribe
    is blind!"

Straight on that glittering ice-field, by the caves of
    the lost Dordogne,
Ung, a maker of pictures, fell to his scribing on
    bone—
Even to mammoth editions.   Gaily he whistled
    and sung,
Blessing his tribe for their blindness.   *Heed ye the*
    Story of Ung!

THE THREE–DECKER.

"The three-volume novel is extinct."

FULL thirty foot she towered from waterline to
    rail.
It cost a watch to steer her, and a week to shorten
    sail;
But, spite all modern notions, I found her first and
    best—
The only certain packet for the Islands of the
    Blest.

Fair held our breeze behind us—'twas warm with
    lovers' prayers:
We'd stolen wills for ballast and a crew of missing
    heirs;
They shipped as Able Bastards till the Wicked
    Nurse confessed,
And they worked the old three-decker to the
    Islands of the Blest.

Carambas and *serapés* we waved to every wind,
We smoked good Corpo Bacco when our sweet-
hearts proved unkind;
With maids of matchless beauty and parentage
unguessed
We also took our manners to the Islands of the
Blest.

We asked no social questions—we pumped no
hidden shame—
We never talked obstetrics when the little stranger
came:
We left the Lord in Heaven, we left the fiends in
Hell.
We weren't exactly Yussufs, but—Zuleika didn't
tell!

No moral doubt assailed us, so when the port we
neared,
The villain got his flogging at the gangway, and
we cheered.
'Twas fiddles in the foc'sle—'twas garlands on the
mast,
For every one got married, and I went ashore at
last.

I left 'em all in couples akissing on the decks.
I left the lovers loving and the parents signing
    checks.
In endless English comfort by county-folk ca-
    ressed,
I left the old three-decker at the Islands of the
    Blest!

That route is barred to steamers: you'll never lift
    again
Our purple-painted headlands or the lordly keeps
    of Spain.
They're just beyond the skyline, howe'er so far you
    cruise
In a ram-you-damn-you liner with a brace of
    bucking screws.

Swing round your aching search-light—'twill show
    no haven's peace!
Ay, blow your shrieking sirens to the deaf, gray-
    bearded seas!
Boom out the dripping oil-bags to skin the deep's
    unrest—
But you aren't a knot the nearer to the Islands
    of the Blest.

And when you're threshing, crippled, with broken
   bridge and rail,
On a drogue of dead convictions to hold you head
   to gale,
Calm as the Flying Dutchman, from truck to taff-
   rail dressed,
You'll see the old three-decker for the Islands of
   the Blest.

You'll see her tiering canvas in sheeted silver
   spread;
You'll hear the long-drawn thunder 'neath her
   leaping figure-head;
While far, so far above you, her tall poop-lanterns
   shine
Unvexed by wind or weather like the candles
   round a shrine.

Hull down—hull down and under—she dwindles
   to a speck,
With noise of pleasant music and dancing on her
   deck.
All's well—all's well aboard her—she's dropped
   you far behind,
With a scent of old-world roses through the fog
   that ties you blind.

9

Her crew are babes or madmen ? Her port is all
     to make ?
You're manned by Truth and Science, and you
     steam for steaming's sake ?
Well, tinker up your engines—you know your
     business best—
She's taking tired people to the Islands of the
     Blest!

AN AMERICAN.

The American Spirit speaks:

If the Led Striker call it a strike,
    Or the papers call it a war,
They know not much what I am like,
    Nor what he is, my Avatar.

Through many roads, by me possessed,
    He shambles forth in cosmic guise;
He is the Jester and the Jest,
    And he the Text himself applies.

The Celt is in his heart and hand,
    The Gaul is in his brain and nerve;
Where, cosmopolitanly planned,
    He guards the Redskin's dry reserve.

His easy unswept hearth he lends
    From Labrador to Guadeloupe;
Till, elbowed out by sloven friends,
    He camps, at sufferance, on the stoop.

123

Calm-eyed he scoffs at sword and crown,
 Or panic-blinded stabs and slays:
Blatant he bids the world bow down,
 Or cringing begs a crumb of praise;

Or, sombre-drunk, at mine and mart,
 He dubs his dreary brethren Kings.
His hands are black with blood: his heart
 Leaps, as a babe's, at little things.

But, through the shift of mood and mood,
 Mine ancient humour saves him whole—
The cynic devil in his blood
 That bids him mock his hurrying soul;

That bids him flout the Law he makes,
 That bids him make the Law he flouts,
Till, dazed by many doubts, he wakes
 The drumming guns that—have no doubts;

That checks him foolish hot and fond,
 That chuckles through his deepest ire,
That gilds the slough of his despond
 But dims the goal of his desire;

Inopportune, shrill-accented,
    The acrid Asiatic mirth
That leaves him careless 'mid his dead,
    The scandal of the elder earth.

How shall he clear himself, how reach
    Our bar or weighed defence prefer—
A brother hedged with alien speech
    And lacking all interpreter?

Which knowledge vexes him a space;
    But while reproof around him rings,
He turns a keen untroubled face
    Home, to the instant need of things.

Enslaved, illogical, elate,
    He greets th' embarrassed Gods, nor fears
To shake the iron hand of Fate
    Or match with Destiny for beers.

Lo! imperturbable he rules,
    Unkempt, disreputable, vast—
And, in the teeth of all the schools
    I—I shall save him at the last!

THE MARY GLOSTER.

I'VE paid for your sickest fancies; I've humoured
    your crackedest whim—
Dick, it's your daddy—dying: you've got to listen
    to him!
Good for a fortnight, am I? The doctor told you?
    He lied.
I shall go under by morning, and—— Put that
    nurse outside.
'Never seen death yet, Dickie? Well, now is
    your time to learn,
And you'll wish you held my record before it
    comes to your turn.
Not counting the Line and the Foundry, the yards
    and the village, too,
I've made myself and a million; but I'm damned
    if I made you.
Master at two-and-twenty, and married at twenty
    three—

Ten thousand men on the pay-roll, and forty freighters at sea!

Fifty years between 'em, and every year of it fight,

And now I'm Sir Anthony Gloster, dying, a baronite:

For I lunched with His Royal 'Ighness—what was it the papers a-had?

"Not least of our merchant-princes." Dickie, that's me, your dad!

I didn't begin with askings. *I* took my job and I stuck;

And I took the chances they wouldn't, an' now they're calling it luck.

Lord, what boats I've handled—rotten and leaky and old!

Ran 'em, or—opened the bilge-cock, precisely as I was told.

Grub that 'ud bind you crazy, and crews that 'ud turn you gray,

And a big fat lump of insurance to cover the risk on the way.

The others they duresn't do it; they said they valued their life

(They've served me since as skippers). *I* went, and I took my wife.

Over the world I drove 'em, married at twenty-
three,

And your mother saving the money and making a
man of me.

I was content to be master, but she said there was
better behind;

She took the chances I wouldn't, and I followed
your mother blind.

She egged me to borrow the money, an' she
helped me clear the loan,

When we bought half shares in a cheap 'un and
hoisted a flag of our own.

Patching and coaling on credit, and living the Lord
knew how,

We started the Red Ox freighters—we've eight-
and-thirty now.

And those were the days of clippers, and the
freights were clipper-freights,

And we knew we were making our fortune, but
she died in Macassar Straits—

By the Little Paternosters, as you come to the
Union Bank—

And we dropped her in fourteen fathom; I pricked
it off where she sank.

Owners we were, full owners, and the boat was
christened for her,

And she died out there in childbed. My heart,
how young we were!

So I went on a spree round Java and well-nigh ran
her ashore,

But your mother came and warned me and I
wouldn't liquor no more.

Strict I stuck to my business, afraid to stop or I'd
think,

Saving the money (she warned me), and letting
the other men drink.

And I met McCullough in London (I'd saved five
'undred then),

And 'tween us we started the Foundry—three
forges and twenty men:

Cheap repairs for the cheap 'uns. It paid, and the
business grew,

For I bought me a steam-lathe patent, and that
was a gold mine too.

"Cheaper to build 'em than buy 'em," *I* said, but
McCullough he shied,

And we wasted a year in talking before we moved
to the Clyde.

And the Lines were all beginning, and we all of
us started fair,

Building our engines like houses and staying the
boilers square.

But McCullough 'e wanted cabins with marble
     and maple and all,
And Brussels and Utrecht velvet, and baths and a
     Social Hall,
And pipes for closets all over, and cutting the
     frames too light.
But McCullough he died in the Sixties, and——
     Well, I'm dying to-night. . . .
I knew—*I* knew what was coming, when we bid
     on the *Byfleet's* keel.
They piddled and piffled with iron: I'd given my
     orders for steel.
Steel and the first expansions.   It paid, I tell you,
     it paid,
When we came with our nine-knot freighters and
     collared the long-run trade.
And they asked me how I did it, and I gave 'em
     the Scripture text,
"You keep your light so shining a little in front o'
     the next!"
They copied all they could follow, but they couldn't
     copy my mind,
And I left 'em sweating and stealing a year and a
     half behind.
Then came the armour-contracts, but that was
     McCullough's side;

He was always best in the Foundry, but better, perhaps, he died.

I went through his private papers; the notes was plainer than print;

And I'm no fool to finish if a man'll give me a hint.

(I remember his widow was angry.) So I saw what the drawings meant,

And I started the six-inch rollers, and it paid me sixty per cent.

Sixty per cent *with* failures, and more than twice we could do,

And a quarter-million to credit, and I saved it all for you.

I thought—it doesn't matter—you seemed to favour your ma,

But you're nearer forty than thirty, and I know the kind you are.

Harrer an' Trinity College! I ought to ha' sent you to sea—

But I stood you an education, an' what have you done for me?

The things I knew was proper you wouldn't thank me to give,

And the things I knew was rotten you said was the way to live;

For you muddled with books and pictures, an'
china an' etchin's an' fans,

And your rooms at college was beastly—more like
a whore's than a man's—

Till you married that thin-flanked woman, as
white and as stale as a bone,

And she gave you your social nonsense; but
where's that kid o' your own?

I've seen your carriages blocking the half of the
Cromwell Road,

But never the doctor's brougham to help the
missus unload.

(So there isn't even a grandchild, an' the Gloster
family's done.)

Not like your mother, she isn't. *She* carried her
freight each run.

But they died, the pore little beggars! At sea she
had 'em—they died.

Only you, an' you stood it; you haven't stood
much beside—

Weak, a liar, and idle, and mean as a collier's
whelp

Nosing for scraps in the galley. No help—my son
was no help!

So he gets three 'undred thousand, in trust and
the interest paid.

I wouldn't give it you, Dickie—you see, I made it in trade.

You're saved from soiling your fingers, and if you have no child,

It all comes back to the business. Gad, won't your wife be wild!

Calls and calls in her carriage, her 'andkerchief up to 'er eye:

"Daddy! dear daddy's dyin'!" and doing her best to cry.

Grateful? Oh, yes, I'm grateful, but keep 'er away from here.

Your mother 'ud never ha' stood 'er, and, anyhow, women are queer. . . .

There's women will say I've married a second time. Not quite!

But give pore Aggie a hundred, and tell her your lawyers'll fight.

She was the best o' the boiling—you'll meet her before it ends;

I'm in for a row with the mother—I'll leave you settle my friends:

For a man he must go with a woman, which women don't understand—

Or the sort that say they can see it they aren't the marrying brand.

But I wanted to speak o' your mother that's Lady
  Gloster still.

I'm going to up and see her, without it's hurt-
  ing the will.

Here! Take your hand off the bell-pull. Five
  thousand's waiting for you,

If you'll only listen a minute, and do as I bid
  you do.

They'll try to prove me a loony, and, if you
  bungle, they can;

And I've only you to trust to! (O God, why
  ain't he a man ?)

There's some waste money on marbles, the same
  as McCullough tried—

Marbles and mausoleums—but I call that sinful
  pride.

There's some ship bodies for burial—we've carried
  'em, soldered and packed;

Down in their wills they wrote it, and nobody
  called *them* cracked.

But me—I've too much money, and people might.
  . . . All my fault:

It come o' hoping for grandsons and buying that
  Wokin' vault.

I'm sick o' the 'ole dam' business; I'm going back
  where I came.

Dick, you're the son o' my body, and you'll take
    charge o' the same!
I'm going to lie by your mother, ten thousand mile
    away,
And they'll want to send me to Woking; and that's
    where you'll earn your pay.
I've thought it out on the quiet, the same as it
    ought to be done—
Quiet, and decent, and proper—an' here's your
    orders, my son.
You know the Line? You don't, though. You
    write to the Board, and tell
Your father's death has upset you an' you're goin'
    to cruise for a spell,
An' you'd like the Mary Gloster—I've held her
    ready for this—
They'll put her in working order an' you'll take
    her out as she is.
Yes, it was money idle when I patched her and put
    her aside
(Thank God, I can pay for my fancies!)—the boat
    where your mother died,
By the Little Paternosters, as you come to the
    Union Bank,
We dropped her—I think I told you—and I pricked
    it off where she sank.

[Tiny she looked on the grating—that oily, treacly
     sea—]

Hundred and eighteen East, remember, and South
     just three.

Easy bearings to carry—three South—three to the
     dot;

But I gave McAndrews a copy in case of dying—or
     not.

And so you'll write to McAndrews, he's Chief of
     the Maori Line;

They'll give him leave, if you ask 'em and say it's
     business o' mine.

I built three boats for the Maoris, an' very well
     pleased they were,

An' I've known Mac since the Fifties, and Mac knew
     me—and her.

After the first stroke warned me I sent him the
     money to keep

Against the time you'd claim it, committin' your
     dad to the deep;

For you are the son o' my body, and Mac was my
     oldest friend,

I've never asked 'im to dinner, but he'll see it out
     to the end.

Stiff-necked Glasgow beggar, I've heard he's
     prayed for my soul,

But he couldn't lie if you paid him, and he'd starve
    before he stole.

He'll take the Mary in ballast—you'll find her a
    lively ship;

And you'll take Sir Anthony Gloster, that goes on
    his wedding-trip,

Lashed in our old deck-cabin with all three port-
    holes wide,

The kick o' the screw beneath him and the round
    blue seas outside!

Sir Anthony Gloster's carriage—our 'ouse-flag fly-
    in' free—

Ten thousand men on the pay-roll and forty
    freighters at sea!

He made himself and a million, but this world is
    a fleetin' show,

And he'll go to the wife of 'is bosom the same as
    he ought to go.

By the heel of the Paternosters—there isn't a chance
    to mistake—

And Mac'll pay you the money as soon as the bub-
    bles break!

Five thousand for six weeks' cruising, the stanch-
    est freighter afloat,

And Mac he'll give you your bonus the minute I'm
    out o' the boat!

    10

He'll take you round to Macassar, and you'll come
    back alone;

He knows what I want o' the Mary. . . . I'll do
    what I please with my own.

Your mother 'ud call it wasteful, but I've seven-
    and-thirty more;

I'll come in my private carriage and bid it wait at
    the door. . . .

For my son 'e was never a credit: 'e muddled
    with books and art,

And 'e lived on Sir Anthony's money and 'e broke
    Sir Anthony's heart.

There isn't even a grandchild, and the Gloster
    family's done—

The only one you left me, O mother, the only
    one!

Harrer an' Trinity College! Me slavin' early an'
    late,

An' he thinks I'm dyin' crazy, and you're in Ma-
    cassar Strait!

Flesh o' my flesh, my dearie, for ever an' ever
    amen,

That first stroke come for a warning; I ought to
    ha' gone to you then,

But—cheap repairs for a cheap 'un—the doctors
    said I'd do:

Mary, why didn't *you* warn me ?   I've allus heeded
to you,

Excep'—I know—about women; but you are a
spirit now;

An', wife, they was only women, and I was a man.
That's how.

An' a man 'e must go with a woman, as you could
not understand;

But I never talked 'em secrets.   I paid 'em out o'
hand.

Thank Gawd, I can pay for my fancies!   Now
what's five thousand to me,

For a berth off the Paternosters in the haven where
I would be ?

I believe in the Resurrection, if I read my Bible
plain,

But I wouldn't trust 'em at Wokin'; we're safer at
sea again.

For the heart it shall go with the treasure—go
down to the sea in ships.

I'm sick of the hired women—I'll kiss my girl on
her lips!

I'll be content with my fountain, I'll drink from my
own well,

And the wife of my youth shall charm me—an' the
rest can go to Hell!

(Dickie, *he* will, that's certain.)   I'll lie in our
  standin'-bed,
An' Mac'll take her in ballast—and she trims best
  by the head. . . .
Down by the head an' sinkin'.   Her fires are drawn
  and cold,
And the water's splashin' hollow on the skin of
  the empty hold—
Churning an' choking and chuckling, quiet and
  scummy and dark—
Full to her lower hatches and risin' steady.
  Hark!
That was the after-bulkhead. . . . she's flooded
  from stem to stern. . . .
Never seen death yet, Dickie? . . . Well, now is
  your time to learn!

SESTINA OF THE TRAMP-ROYAL.

Speakin' in general, I 'ave tried 'em all,
The 'appy roads that take you o'er the world.
Speakin' in general, I 'ave found them good
For such as cannot use one bed too long,
But must get 'ence, the same as I 'ave done,
An' go observin' matters till they die.

What do it matter where or 'ow we die,
So long as we've our 'ealth to watch it all—
The different ways that different things are done,
An' men an' women lovin' in this world—
Takin' our chances as they come along,
An' when they ain't, pretendin' they are good?

In cash or credit—no, it ain't no good;
You 'ave to 'ave the 'abit or you'd die,
Unless you lived your life but one day long,
Nor didn't prophesy nor fret at all,
But drew your tucker some'ow from the world,
An' never bothered what you might ha' done.

But, Gawd, what things are they I 'aven't done?
I've turned my 'and to most, an' turned it good,
In various situations round the world—
For 'im that doth not work must surely die;
But that's no reason man should labour all
'Is life on one same shift; life's none so long.

Therfore, from job to job I've moved along.
Pay couldn't 'old me when my time was done,
For something in my 'ead upset me all,
Till I 'ad dropped whatever 'twas for good,
An', out at sea, be'eld the dock-lights die,
An' met my mate—the wind that tramps the world.

It's like a book, I think, this bloomin' world,
Which you can read and care for just so long,
But presently you feel that you will die
Unless you get the page you're readin' done,
An' turn another—likely not so good;
But what you're after is to turn 'em all.

Gawd bless this world! Whatever she 'ath done—
Excep' when awful long—I've found it good.
So write, before I die, "'E liked it all!"

BARRACK-ROOM BALLADS.

When 'Omer smote 'is bloomin' lyre,
  He'd 'eard men sing by land an' sea;
An' what he thought 'e might require,
  'E went an' took—the same as me!

The market-girls an' fishermen,
  The shepherds an' the sailors, too,
They 'eard old songs turn up again,
  But kep' it quiet—same as you!

They knew 'e stole; 'e knew they knowed.
  They didn't tell, nor make a fuss,
But winked at 'Omer down the road,
  An' 'e winked back—the same as us!

"BACK TO THE ARMY AGAIN."

I'M 'ere in a ticky ulster an' a broken billycock 'at,
A-layin' on to the sergeant I don't know a gun
     from a bat;
My shirt's doin' duty for jacket, my sock's stickin'
     out o' my boots,
An' I'm learnin' the damned old goose-step along
     o' the new recruits!

  Back to the Army again, sergeant,
    Back to the Army again.
  Don't look so 'ard, for I 'aven't no card,
    I'm back to the Army again!

I done my six years' service. 'Er Majesty sez:
     "Good day—
You'll please to come when you're rung for, an'
     'ere's your 'ole back pay;
An' four-pence a day for baccy—an' bloomin' gen-
     'rous, too;
An' now you can make your fortune—the same as
     your orf'cers do."

Back to the Army again, sergeant,
    Back to the Army again;
'Ow did I learn to do right-about turn?
    I'm back to the army again!

A man o' four-an'-twenty that 'asn't learned of a
        trade—
Beside "Reserve" agin' him—'e'd better be never
        made.
I tried my luck for a quarter, an' that was enough
        for me,
An' I thought of 'Er Majesty's barricks, an' I
        thought I'd go an' see.

Back to the Army again, sergeant,
    Back to the Army again;
'Tisn't my fault if I dress when I 'alt—
    I'm back to the Army again!

The sergeant arst no questions, but 'e winked the
        other eye,
E' sez to me, "'Shun!" an' I shunted, the same
        as in days gone by;
For 'e saw the set o' my shoulders, an' I couldn't
        'elp 'oldin' straight
When me an' the other rookies come under the
        barrick gate.

Back to the Army again, sergeant,
 Back to the Army again;
'Oo would ha' thought I could carry an' port?
 I'm back to the Army again!

I took my bath, an' I wallered—for, Gawd, I
  needed it so!
I smelt the smell o' the barricks, I 'eard the bugles
  go.
I 'eard the feet on the gravel—the feet o' the men
  what drill—
An' I sez to my flutterin' 'eart-strings, I sez to 'em,
  "Peace, be still!"

 Back to the Army again, sergeant,
  Back to the Army again;
 'Oo said I knew when the Jumner was due?
  I'm back to the Army again!

I carried my slops to the tailor; I sez to 'im,
  "None o' your lip!
You tight 'em over the shoulders, an' loose 'em
  over the 'ip,
For the set o' the tunic's 'orrid." An' 'e sez to me,
  "Strike me dead,
But I thought you was used to the business!" an'
  so 'e done what I said.

Back to the Army again, sergeant,
  Back to the Army again.
Rather too free with my fancies? Wot—me?
  I'm back to the Army again!

Next week I'll 'ave 'em fitted; I'll buy me a walk-
      in' cane;
They'll let me free o' the barricks to walk on the
      Hoe again
In the name o' William Parsons, that used to be
      Edward Clay,
An'—any pore beggar that wants it can draw my
      fourpence a day!

Back to the Army again, sergeant,
  Back to the Army again:
Out o' the cold an' the rain, sergeant,
  Out o' the cold an' the rain.

            'Oo's there?
A man that's too good to be lost you,
  A man that is 'andled an' made—
A man that will pay what 'e cost you
  In learnin' the others their trade—parade!
You're droppin' the pick o' the Army
  Because you don't 'elp 'em remain,
But drives 'em to cheat to get out o' the street
  An' back to the Army again!

"BIRDS OF PREY" MARCH.

MARCH!   The mud is cakin' good about our
    trousies.
  Front!—eyes front, an' watch the Colour-casin's
    drip.
Front!   The faces of the women in the 'ouses
    Ain't the kind o' things to take aboard the ship.

Cheer ! An' we'll never march to victory.
Cheer ! An' we'll never live to 'ear the cannon
    roar !
        The Large Birds o' Prey
        They will carry us away,
An' you'll never see your soldiers any more !

Wheel!   Oh, keep your touch; we're goin' round
    a corner.
  Time!—mark time, an' let the men be'ind us
    close.

Lord! the transport's full, an' 'alf our lot not on
    'er—
  Cheer, O cheer! We're going off where no
    one knows.

March! The Devil's none so black as 'e is
    painted!
  Cheer! We'll 'ave some fun before we're put
    away.
'Alt, an' 'and 'er out—a woman's gone and
    fainted!
  Cheer! Get on—Gawd 'elp the married men
    to-day!

Hoi! Come up, you 'ungry beggars, to yer sor-
    row.
  ('Ear them say they want their tea, an' want it
    quick!)
You won't have no mind for slingers, not to-mor-
    row—
  No; you'll put the 'tween-decks stove out, bein'
    sick!

'Alt! The married kit 'as all to go before us!
  'Course it's blocked the bloomin' gangway up
    again!

Cheer, O cheer the 'Orse Guards watchin' tender
o'er us,
Keepin' us since eight this mornin' in the rain!

Stuck in 'eavy marchin'-order, sopped and wring-
in'—
Sick, before our time to watch 'er 'eave an' fall,
'Ere's your 'appy 'ome at last, an' stop your sing-
in'.
'Alt! Fall in along the troop-deck! Silence all!

Cheer! For we'll never live to see no bloom-
in' victory!
Cheer! An' we'll never live to' ear the cannon
roar! (One cheer more!)
The jackal an' the kite
'Ave an 'ealthy appetite,
An' you'll never see your soldiers any more!
('Ip! Urroar!)
The eagle an' the crow
They are waitin' ever so,
An' you'll never see your soldiers any more!
('Ip! Urroar!)
Yes, the Large Birds o' Prey
They will carry us away,
An' you'll never see your soldiers any more!

"SOLDIER AN' SAILOR TOO."

As I was spittin' into the Ditch aboard o' the Croc-
      odile,
I seed a man on a man-o'-war got up in the
      Reg'lars' style.
'E was scrapin' the paint from off of 'er plates, an'
      I sez to 'im, "'Oo are you?"
Sez 'e, "I'm a Jolly—'Er Majesty's Jolly—soldier
      an' sailor too!"
Now 'is work begins at Gawd knows when, and
      'is work is never through;
'E isn't one o' the reg'lar Line, nor 'e isn't one of
      the crew.
'E's a kind of a giddy harumfrodite—soldier an'
      sailor too!

An' after I met 'im all over the world, a-doin' all
      kinds of things,
Like landin' 'isself with a Gatlin' gun to talk to
      them 'eathen kings;

'E sleeps in an 'ammick instead of a cot, an' 'e
   drills with the deck on a slew,
An' 'e sweats like a Jolly—'Er Majesty's Jolly—soldier an' sailor too!
For there isn't a job on the top o' the earth the
   beggar don't know, nor do.
You can leave 'im at night on a bald man's 'ead,
   to paddle 'is own canoe;
'E's a sort of a bloomin' cosmopolouse—soldier an'
   sailor too.

We've fought 'em on trooper, we've fought 'em
   in dock, an' drunk with 'em in betweens,
When they called us the seasick scull'ry maids,
   an' we called 'em the Ass Marines;
But, when we was down for a double fatigue, from
   Woolwich to Bernardmyo,
We sent for the Jollies—'Er Majesty's Jollies—sol-
   dier an' sailor too!
They think for 'emselves, an' they steal for 'em-
   selves, and they never ask what's to do,
But they're camped an' fed an' they're up an' fed
   before our bugle's blew.
Ho! they ain't no limpin' procrastitutes—soldier
   an' sailor too.

   11

You may say we are fond of an 'arness-cut, or
 'ootin' in barrick-yards,
Or startin' a Board School mutiny along o' the
 Onion Guards;
But once in a while we can finish in style for the
 ends of the earth to view,
The same as the Jollies—'er Majesty's Jollies—sol-
 dier an' sailor too !
They come of our lot, they was brothers to us;
 they was beggars we'd met an' knew;
Yes, barrin' an inch in the chest an' the arms, they
 was doubles o' me an' you;
For they weren't no special chrysanthemums—
 soldier an' sailor too!

To take your chance in the thick of a rush, with
 firing all about,
Is nothing so bad when you've cover to 'and, an'
 leave an' likin' to shout;
But to stand an' be still to the *Birken'ead* drill is a
 damn tough bullet to chew,
An' they done it, the Jollies—'Er Majesty's Jollies
 —soldier an' sailor too!
Their work was done when it 'adn't begun; they
 was younger nor me an' you;

Their choice it was plain between drownin' in
    'eaps an' bein' mashed by the screw,
So they stood an' was still to the *Birken'ead* drill,
    soldier an' sailor too!

We're most of us liars, we're 'arf of us thieves, an'
    the rest are as rank as can be,
But once in a while we can finish in style (which
    I 'ope it won't 'appen to me).
But it makes you think better o' you an' your
    friends, an' the work you may 'ave to do,
When you think o' the sinkin' *Victorier's* Jollies—
    soldier an' sailor too!
Now there isn't no room for to say ye don't
    know—they 'ave proved it plain and true—
That whether it's Widow, or whether it's ship,
    Victorier's work is to do,
An' they done it, the Jollies—'Er Majesty's Jollies—
    soldier an' sailor too!

SAPPERS.

When the Waters were dried an' the Earth did appear
    ("It's all one," says the Sapper),
The Lord He created the Engineer,
    Her Majesty's Royal Engineer,
    With the rank and pay of a Sapper!

When the Flood come along for an extra monsoon,
'Twas Noah constructed the first pontoon
    To the plans of Her Majesty's, etc.

But after "fatigue" in the wet an' the sun,
Old Noah got drunk, which he wouldn't ha' done
    If he'd trained with, etc.

When the Tower o' Babel had mixed up men's *bat*,
Some clever civilian was managing that,
    An' none of, etc.

When the Jews had a fight at the foot of an 'ill,
Young Joshua ordered the sun to stand still,
   For he was a Captain of Engineers, etc.

When the Children of Israel made bricks without
    straw,
They were learnin' the regular work of our Corps,
   The work of, etc.

For ever since then, if a war they would wage,
Behold us a-shinin' on history's page—
   First page for, etc.

We lay down their sidings an' help 'em entrain,
An' we sweep up their mess through the bloomin'
    campaign,
   In the style of, etc.

They send us in front with a fuse an' a mine
To blow up the gates that are rushed by the
    Line,
   But bent by, etc.

They send us behind with a pick an' a spade,
To dig for the guns of a bullock-brigade
   Which has asked for, etc.

We work under escort in trousies an' shirt,
An' the heathen they plug us tail-up in the dirt,
    Annoying, etc.

We blast out the rock an' we shovel the mud,
We make 'em good roads an'—they roll down the
    khud,
    Reporting, etc.

We make 'em their bridges, their wells, an' their
    huts,
An' the telegraph-wire the enemy cuts,
    An' it's blamed on, etc.

An' when we return an' from war we would
    cease,
They grudge us adornin' the billets of peace,
    Which are kept for, etc.

We build 'em nice barricks—they swear they
    are bad,
That our Colonels are Methodist, married or
    mad,
    Insultin', etc.

They haven't no manners nor gratitude too,
For the more that we help 'em the less will they
do,
But mock at, etc.

Now the Line's but a man with a gun in his
hand,
An' Cavalry's only what horses can stand,
When helped by, etc.

Artillery moves by the leave o' the ground,
But *we* are the men that do something all round,
For *we* are, etc.

I have stated it plain, an' my argument's thus,
("It's all one," says the Sapper),
There's only one Corps which is perfect—that's
us;
An' they call us Her Majesty's Engineers,
Her Majesty's Royal Engineers,
With the rank and pay of a Sapper!

THAT DAY.

It got beyond all orders an' it got beyond
    all 'ope;
  It got to shammin' wounded an' retirin' from
    the 'alt.
'Ole companies was lookin' for the nearest road to
    slope;
  It were just a bloomin' knock-out—an' our
    fault!

Now there ain't no chorus 'ere to give,
* Nor there ain't no band to play;*
An' I wish I was dead 'fore I done what I did
* Or seen what I seed that day!*

We was sick o' bein' punished, an' we let 'em
    know it, too;
  An' a company-commander up an' 'it us with a
    sword,

An' some one shouted "'Ook it!" an' it come to
    sove-ki-poo,
  An' we chucked our rifles from us—oh, my
    Gawd!

There was thirty dead an' wounded on the ground
    we wouldn't keep—
  No, there wasn't more than twenty when the
    front begun to go;
But, Christ! along the line o' flight they cut us up
    like sheep,
  An' that was all we gained by doin' so.

I 'eard the knives be'ind me, but I dursn't face my
    man,
  An' I don't know where I went to, 'cause I
    didn't 'alt to see,
Till I 'eard a beggar squealin' out for quarter as 'e
    ran,
  An' I thought I knew the voice an'—it was me!

We was 'idin' under bedsteads more than 'arf a
    march away;
  We was lyin' up like rabbits all about the coun-
    try side;

An' the major cursed 'is Maker 'cause 'e lived to
     see that day,
  An' the colonel broke 'is sword acrost, an'
     cried.

We was rotten 'fore we started—we was never
     disci*plined*;
  We made it out a favour if an order was
     obeyed;
Yes, every little drummer 'ad 'is rights an' wrongs
     to mind,
  So we had to pay for teachin'—an' we paid!

The papers 'id it 'andsome, but you know the
     Army knows;
  We was put to groomin' camels till the regi-
     ments withdrew,
An' they give us each a medal for subduin' Eng-
     land's foes,
  An' I 'ope you like my song—because it's true!

An' there ain't no chorus 'ere to give,
  Nor there ain't no band to play;
But I wish I was dead 'fore I done what I did
  Or seen what I seed that day!

"THE MEN THAT FOUGHT AT MINDEN."

A SONG OF INSTRUCTION.

The men that fought at Minden, they was rookies
    in their time—
    So was them that fought at Waterloo!
All the 'ole command, yuss, from Minden to Mai-
    wand,
    They was once dam' sweeps like you!

*Then do not be discouraged, 'Eaven is your
    'elper,
    We'll learn you not to forget;
An' you mustn't swear an' curse, or you'll only
    catch it worse,
    For we'll make you soldiers yet.*

The men that fought at Minden, they 'ad stocks
    beneath their chins,
    Six inch 'igh an' more;

But fatigue it was their pride, and they *would* not
      be denied
    To clean the cook-'ouse floor.

The men that fought at Minden, they 'ad anarch-
      istic bombs
    Served to 'em by name of 'and-grenades;
But they got it in the eye (same as you will by
      an' by)
    When they clubbed their field-parades.

The men that fought at Minden, they 'ad buttons
      up an' down,
   Two-an'-twenty dozen of 'em told;
But they didn't grouse an' shirk at an hour's extry
      work,
    They kept 'em bright as gold.

The men that fought at Minden, they was armed
      with musketoons,
    Also, they was drilled by 'alberdiers;
I don't know what they were, but the sergeants
      took good care
    They washed be'ind their ears.

The men that fought at Minden, they 'ad ever cash
  in 'and
    Which they did not bank nor save,
But spent it gay an' free on their betters—such as
  me—
    For the good advice I gave.

The men that fought at Minden, they was civil
    —yuss, they was—
    Never didn't talk o' rights an' wrongs,
But they got it with the toe (same as you will get
  it—so!)—
    For interrupting songs.

The men that fought at Minden, they was several
  other things
    Which I don't remember clear;
But *that's* the reason why, now the six-year men
  are dry,
    The rooks will stand the beer!

  *Then do not be discouraged, 'Eaven is your
    'elper,*
    We'll learn you not to forget;
  *An' you mustn't swear an' curse, or you'll only
    catch it worse,*
    And we'll make you soldiers yet.

Soldiers yet, if you've got it in you—
  All for the sake o' the Core;
Soldiers yet, if we 'ave to skin you—
  Run an' get the beer, Johnny Raw—Johnny
    Raw!
  Ho! run an' get the beer, Johnny Raw!

CHOLERA CAMP.

WE'VE got the cholerer in camp—it's worse than
     forty fights;
We're dyin' in the wilderness the same as Isru-
     lites!
It's before us, an' be'ind us, an' we cannot get
     away,
An' the doctor's just reported we've ten more
     to-day!

    Oh, strike your camp an' go, the bugle's callin',
       The Rains are fallin'—
    The dead are bushed an' stoned to keep 'em safe
       below ;
    The Band's a-doin' all she knows to cheer us ;
    The chaplain's gone and prayed to Gawd to
       'ear us—
       To 'ear us—
    O Lord, for it's a-killing of us so !

Since August, when it started, it's been sticking to
　　our tail,
Tho' they've 'ad us out by marches an' they've
　　'ad us back by rail;
But it runs as fast as troop-trains, an' we can not
　　get away;
An' the sick-list to the Colonel makes ten more
　　to-day.

There ain't no fun in women nor there ain't no bite
　　to drink;
It's much too wet for shootin', we can only march
　　and think;
An' at evenin', down the *nullahs*, we can 'ear
　　the jackals say,
"Get up, you rotten beggars, you've ten more
　　to-day!"

'Twould make a monkey cough to see our way
　　o' doin' things—
Lieutenants takin' companies an' captains takin'
　　wings,
An' Lances actin' Sergeants—eight file to obey—
For we've lot's o' quick promotion on ten
　　deaths a day!

Our Colonel's white an' twitterly—'e gets no sleep
    nor food,
But mucks about in 'orspital where nothing does
    no good.
'E sends us 'eaps o' comforts, all bought from 'is
    pay—
But there aren't much comfort 'andy on ten deaths
    a day.

Our Chaplain's got a banjo, an' a skinny mule 'e
    rides,
An' the stuff 'e says an' sings us, Lord, it makes
    us split our sides!
With 'is black coat-tails a-bobbin' to *Ta-ra-ra*
    Boom-der-ay!
'E's the proper kind o' *padre* for ten deaths a
    day.

An' Father Victor 'elps 'im with our Roman Catho-
    licks—
He knows an 'eap of Irish songs an' rummy con-
    jurin' tricks;
An' the two they works together when it comes
    to play or pray;
So we keep the ball a-rollin' on ten deaths a
    day.
    12

We've got the cholerer in camp—we've got it 'ot
    an' sweet;
It ain't no Christmas dinner, but it's 'elped an' we
    must eat.
We've gone beyond the funkin', 'cause we've found
    it doesn't pay,
An' we're rockin' round the Districk on ten deaths
    a day!

> Then strike your camp an' go, the Rains are
>   fallin',
>   The bugle's callin'!
> The dead are bushed an' stoned to keep 'em safe
>   below!
> An' them that do not like it they can lump it,
> An' them that can not stand it they can jump it;
> We've got to die somewhere—some way—some-
>   'ow—
> We might as well begin to do it now!
> Then, Number One, let down the tent-pole
>   slow,
> Knock out the pegs an' 'old the corners—so!
> Fold in the flies, furl up the ropes, an' stow!
> Oh, strike—oh, strike your camp an' go!
>   (Gawd 'elp us!)

THE LADIES.

I'VE taken my fun where I've found it;
   I've rogued an' I've ranged in my time;
I've 'ad my pickin' o' sweet'earts,
   An' four o' the lot was prime.
One was an 'arf-caste widow,
   One was a woman at Prome,
One was the wife of a *jemadar-sais,**
   An' one is a girl at 'ome.

Now I aren't no 'and with the ladies,
   For, takin' 'em all along,
You never can say till you've tried 'em,
   An' then you are like to be wrong.
There's times when you'll think that you mightn't,
   There's times when you'll know that you might;
But the things you will learn from the Yellow an'
     Brown,
   They'll 'elp you an 'eap with the White!

---

* Head-groom.

I was a young un at 'Oogli,
    Shy as a girl to begin;
Aggie de Castrer she made me,
    An' Aggie was clever as sin;
Older than me, but my first un—
    More like a mother she were—
Showed me the way to promotion an' pay,
    An' I learned about women from 'er.

Then I was ordered to Burma,
    Actin' in charge o' Bazar,
An' I got me a tiddy live 'eathen
    Through buyin' supplies off 'er pa.
Funny an' yellow an' faithful—
    Doll in a teacup she were,
But we lived on the square, like a true-married
        pair,
    An' I learned about women from 'er.

Then we was shifted to Neemuch
    (Or I might ha' been keepin' 'er now),
An' I took with a shiny she-devil,
    The wife of a nigger at Mhow;

'Taught me the gipsy-folks' *bolee;* *
    Kind o' volcano she were,
For she knifed me one night 'cause I wished she
        was white,
    And I learned about women from 'er.

Then I come 'ome in the trooper,
    'Long of a kid o' sixteen—
Girl from a convent at Meerut,
    The straightest I ever 'ave seen.
Love at first sight was 'er trouble,
    She didn't know what it were;
An' I wouldn't do such, 'cause I liked 'er too much,
    But—I learned about women from 'er!

I've taken my fun where I've found it,
    An' now I must pay for my fun,
For the more you 'ave known o' the others
    The less will you settle to one;
An' the end of it's sittin' and thinkin',
    An' dreamin' Hell-fires to see;
So be warned by my lot (which I know you will
        not),
    An' learn about women from me!

---

* Slang.

What did the colonel's lady think?
   Nobody never knew.
Somebody asked the sergeant's wife,
   An' she told 'em true.
When you get to a man in the case,
   They're like as a row of pins—
For the colonel's lady an' Judy O'Grady
   Are sisters under their skins!

BILL 'AWKINS.

"''As anybody seen Bill 'Awkins?"
  "Now 'ow in the devil would I know?"
"''E's taken my girl out walkin',
    An' I've got to tell 'im so—
        Gawd—bless—'im !
    I've got to tell 'im so."

  "D'yer know what 'e's like, Bill 'Awkins?"
    "Now what in the devil would I care?"
"''E's the livin', breathin' image of an organ-
    grinder's monkey,
    With a pound of grease in 'is 'air—
        Gawd—bless—'im!
    An' a pound o' grease in 'is 'air."

  "An' s'pose you met Bill 'Awkins,
    Now what in the devil 'ud ye do?"

"I'd open 'is cheek to 'is chin-strap buckle,
    An' bung up 'is both eyes, too—
        Gawd—bless—'im!
    An' bung up 'is both eyes, too!"

"Look 'ere, where 'e comes, Bill 'Awkins!
    Now what in the devil will you say?"
"It isn't fit an' proper to be fightin' on a Sunday,
    So I'll pass 'im the time o' day—
        Gawd—bless—'im!
    I'll pass 'im the time o' day!"

THE MOTHER-LODGE.

There was Rundle, Station Master,
    An' Beazeley of the Rail,
An' 'Ackman, Commissariat,
    An' 'Donkin o' the Jail;
An' Blake, Conductor-Sargent,
    Our Master twice was 'e,
With 'im that kept the Europe shop,
    Old Framjee Eduljee.

Outside—" Sergeant! Sir! Salute! Salaam!"
Inside—" Brother," an' it doesn't do no 'arm.
We met upon the Level an' we parted on the
    Square,
An' I was Junior Deacon in my Mother Lodge out
    there!

We'd Bola Nath, Accountant,
    An' Saul the Aden Jew,
An' Din Mohammed, draughtsman
    Of the Survey Office too;

There was Babu Chuckerbutty,
  An' Amir Singh the Sikh,
An' Castro from the fittin'-sheds,
  The Roman Catholick !

We 'adn't good regalia,
  An' our Lodge was old an' bare,
But we knew the Ancient Landmarks,
  An' we kep' 'em to a hair;
An' lookin' on it backwards
  It often strikes me thus,
There ain't such things as infidels,
  Excep', per'aps, it's us.

For monthly, after Labour,
  We'd all sit down and smoke
(We dursn't give no banquits,
  Lest a Brother's caste were broke),
An' man on man got talkin'
  Religion an' the rest,
An' every man comparin'
  Of the God 'e knew the best.

So man on man got talkin',
  An' not a Brother stirred

Till mornin' waked the parrots
   An' that dam' brain-fever-bird;
We'd say 'twas 'ighly curious,
   An' we'd all ride 'ome to bed,
With Mo'ammed, God, an' Shiva
   Changin' pickets in our 'ead.

Full oft on Guv'ment service
   This rovin' foot 'ath pressed,
An' bore fraternal greetin's
   To the Lodges east an' west,
Accordin' as commanded
   From Kohat to Singapore,
But I wish that I might see them
   In my Mother Lodge once more!

I wish that I might see them,
   My Brethren black an' brown,
With the trichies smellin' pleasant
   An' the *hog-darn** passin' down;
An' the old khansamah † snorin'
   On the bottle-khana ‡ floor,
Like a Master in good standing
   With my Mother Lodge once more!

---

* Cigar-lighter.   † Butler.   ‡ Pantry.

Outside—"*Sergeant!   Sir!   Salute!   Salaam!*"
Inside—"*Brother,*" *an' it doesn't do no 'arm.*
We met upon the Level an' we parted on the
      Square,
An' I was Junior Deacon in my Mother Lodge out
      there!

"FOLLOW ME 'OME."

THERE was no one like 'im, 'Orse or Foot,
  Nor any o' the Guns I knew;
An' because it was so, why, o' course 'e went an'
  died,
  Which is just what the best men do.

So it's knock out your pipes an' follow me!
An' it's finish up your swipes an' follow me!
Oh, 'ark to the big drum callin',
Follow me—follow me 'ome!

'Is mare she neighs the 'ole day long,
  She paws the 'ole night through,
An' she won't take 'er feed 'cause o' waitin' for 'is
  step,
  Which is just what a beast would do.

'Is girl she goes with a bombardier
  Before 'er month is through;

181

An' the banns are up in church, for she's got the
        beggar hooked,
        Which is just what a girl would do.

        We fought 'bout a dog—last week it were—
        No more than a round or two;
But I strook 'im cruel 'ard, an' I wish I 'adn't
        now,
        Which is just what a man can't do.

        'E was all that I 'ad in the way of a friend,
        An' I've 'ad to find one new;
But I'd give my pay an' stripe for to get the beggar
        back,
        Which it's just too late to do.

        So it's knock out your pipes an' follow me !
        An' it's finish off your swipes an' follow me !
        Oh, 'ark to the fifes a-crawlin' !
        Follow me—follow me 'ome !

        Take 'im away !   'E's gone where the best
        men go.
        Take 'im away !   An' the gun-wheels
        turnin' slow.

Take 'im away! There's more from the
　　place 'e come.
Take 'im away, with the limber an' the
　　drum.

For it's " Three rounds blank" an' follow me,
An' it's " Thirteen rank" an' follow me ;
　Oh, passin' the love o' women,
　　Follow me—follow me 'ome !

THE SERGEANT'S WEDDIN'.

'E was warned agin 'er—
  That's what made 'im look;
She was warned agin 'im—
  That is why she took.
'Wouldn't 'ear no reason,
  'Went an' done it blind;
We know all about 'em,
  They've got all to find!

    Cheer for the Sergeant's weddin'—
      Give 'em one cheer more!
    Gray gun-'orses in the lando,
      An' a rogue is married to, etc.

What's the use o' tellin'
  'Arf the lot she's been?
'E's a bloomin' robber,
  An' 'e keeps canteen.
'Ow did 'e get 'is buggy?
  Gawd, you needn't ask!
Made 'is forty gallon
  Out of every cask!

Watch 'im, with 'is 'air cut,
    Count us filin' by—
Won't the Colonel praise 'is
    Pop—u—lar—i—ty!
We 'ave scores to settle—
    Scores for more than beer;
She's the girl to pay 'em—
    That is why we're 'ere !

See the chaplain thinkin' ?
    See the women smile ?
Twig the married winkin'
    As they take the aisle ?
Keep your side-arms quiet,
    Dressin' by the Band.
Ho! You 'oly beggars,
    Cough be'ind your 'and!

Now it's done an' over,
    'Ear the organ squeak,
"*Voice that breathed o'er Eden*"—
    Ain't she got the cheek!
White an' laylock ribbons,
    Think yourself so fine!
I'd pray Gawd to take yer
    'Fore I made yer mine!

13

Escort to the kerridge,
    Wish 'im luck, the brute!
Chuck the slippers after—
    [Pity 'taint a boot!]
Bowin' like a lady,
    Blushin' like a lad—
'Oo would say to see 'em—
    Both are rotten bad!

Cheer for the Sergeant's weddin'—
    Give 'em one cheer more!
Gray gun-'orses in the lando,
    An' a rogue is married to, etc.

THE JACKET.

Through the Plagues of Egyp' we was chasin'
    Arabi,
  Gettin' down an' shovin' in the sun;
An' you might 'ave called us dirty, an' you might
    ha' called us dry,
  An' you might 'ave 'eard us talkin' at the gun.
But the Captain 'ad 'is jacket, an' the jacket it
    was new—
  ('Orse-Gunners, listen to my song!)
An' the wettin' of the jacket is the proper thing
    to do,
  Nor we didn't keep 'im waiting very long!

One day they give us orders for to shell a sand re-
    doubt,
  Loadin' down the axle-arms with case;
But the Captain knew 'is dooty, an' he took the
    crackers out,
  An' he put some proper liquor in its place.

An' the Captain saw the shrapnel (which is six-
an'-thirty clear).
    ('Orse-Gunners, listen to my song!)
"Will you draw the weight," sez 'e, "or will you
draw the beer?"
    An' we didn't keep 'im waitin' very long.

    For the Captain, etc.

Then we trotted gentle, not to break the bloomin'
glass,
    Though the Arabites 'ad all their ranges marked;
But we dursn't 'ardly gallop, for the most was
bottled Bass,
    An' we'd dreamed of it since we was disem-
barked.
So we fired economic with the shells we 'ad in 'and,
    ('Orse-Gunners, listen to my song!)
But the beggars under cover 'ad the impidence to
stand,
    An' we couldn't keep 'em waitin' very long.

    And the Captain, etc.

So we finished 'arf the liquor (an' the Captain took
champagne),
    An' the Arabites was shootin' all the while;

An' we left our wounded 'appy with the empties
    on the plain,
  An' we used the bloomin' guns for pro-jec-tile!
We limbered up an' galloped—there were nothin'
    else to do—
  ('Orse-Gunners, listen to my song!)
An' the Battery come a-boundin' like a boundin'
    kangaroo,
  But they didn't watch us comin' very long.

    As the Captain, etc.

We was goin' most extended—we was drivin'
    very fine,
  An' the Arabites were loosin' 'igh an' wide,
Till the Captain took the glassy with a rattlin'
    right incline,
  An' we dropped upon their 'eads the other side.
Then we give 'em quarter—such as 'adn't up and
    cut,
  ('Orse-Gunners, listen to my song!)
An' the Captain stood a limberful of fizzy—some-
    thin' Brutt,
  But we didn't leave it fizzing very long.

    For the Captain, etc.

We might ha' been court-martialled, but it all
　　come out all right
　When they signalled us to join the main com-
　　mand.
There was every round expended, there was every
　　gunner tight,
　An' the Captain waved a corkscrew in 'is 'and!

　　But the Captain had 'is jacket, etc.

THE 'EATHEN.

THE 'eathen in 'is blindness bows down to wood
    an' stone;
'E don't obey no orders unless they is 'is own;
'E keeps 'is side-arms awful: 'e leaves 'em all
    about,
An' then comes up the regiment an' pokes the
    'eathen out.

   All along o' dirtiness, all along o' mess,
   All along o' doin' things rather-more-or-less,
   All along of abby-nay,* kul,† and hazar-ho, ‡
   Mind you keep your rifle an' yourself jus' so!

The young recruit is 'aughty—'e draf's from Gawd
    knows where;
They bid 'im show 'is stockin's an' lay 'is mattress
    square;

---

* Not now.   † To-morrow.   ‡ Wait a bit.

'E calls it bloomin' nonsense—'e doesn't know, no
    more—
An' then up comes 'is company an' kicks 'em
    round the floor!

The young recruit is 'ammered—'e takes it very
    'ard;
'E 'angs 'is 'ead an' mutters—'e sulks about the
    yard;
'E talks o' " cruel tyrants " 'e'll swing for by-an'-
    bye,
An' the others 'ears an' mocks 'im, an' the boy
    goes orf to cry.

The young recruit is silly—'e thinks o' suicide;
'E's lost 'is gutter-devil; 'e 'asn't got 'is pride;
But day by day they kicks 'im, which 'elps 'im on
    a bit,
Till 'e finds 'isself one mornin' with a full an'
    proper kit.

> *Gettin' clear o' dirtiness, gettin' done with*
>   *mess,*
> *Gettin' shut o' doin' things rather-more-or-*
>   *less ;*
> *Not so fond of abby-nay, kul, nor hazar-ho,*
> *Learns to keep 'is rifle an' 'isself jus' so!*

The young recruit is 'appy—'e throws a chest to
suit;
You see 'im grow mustaches; you 'ear 'im slap 'is
boot;
'E learns to drop the "bloodies" from every word
he slings,
An' 'e shows an 'ealthy brisket when 'e strips for
bars an' rings.

The cruel tyrant sergeants they watch 'im 'arf a
year;
They watch 'im with 'is comrades, they watch 'im
with 'is beer;
They watch 'im with the women, at the regi-
mental dance,
And the cruel tyrant sergeants send 'is name along
for "Lance."

An' now 'e's 'arf o' nothin', an' all a private yet,
'Is room they up an' rags 'im to see what they will
get;
They rags 'im low an' cunnin', each dirty trick
they can,
But 'e learns to sweat 'is temper an' 'e learns to
know 'is man.

An', last, a Colour-Sergeant, as such to be
    obeyed,
'E leads 'is men at cricket, 'e leads 'em on parade;
They sees 'em quick an' 'andy, uncommon set an'
    smart,
An' so 'e talks to orficers which 'ave the Core at
    'eart.

'E learns to do 'is watchin' without it showin'
    plain;
'E learns to save a dummy, an' shove 'im straight
    again;
'E learns to check a ranker that's buyin' leave to
    shirk;
An' 'e learns to make men like 'im so they'll learn
    to like their work.

An' when it comes to marchin' he'll see their socks
    are right,
An' when it comes to action 'e shows 'em 'ow to
    sight;
'E knows their ways of thinkin' and just what's in
    their mind;
'E feels when they are comin' on an' when they've
    fell be'ind.

'E knows each talkin' corpril that leads a squad
    astray;
'E feels 'is innards 'eavin', 'is bowels givin'
    way;
'E sees the blue-white faces all tryin' 'ard to
    grin,
An' 'e stands an' waits an' suffers till it's time to
    cap 'em in.

An' now the hugly bullets come peckin' through
    the dust,
An' no one wants to face 'em, but every beggar
    must;
So, like a man in irons which isn't glad to go,
They moves 'em off by companies uncommon
    stiff an' slow.

Of all 'is five years' schoolin' they don't remember
    much
Excep' the not retreatin', the step an' keepin'
    touch.
It looks like teachin' wasted when they duck an'
    spread an' 'op,
But if 'e 'adn't learned 'em they'd be all about the
    shop!

An' now it's "'Oo goes backward ?" an' now it's
      "'Oo comes on ? "
An' now it's " Get the doolies," an' now the
      captain's gone;
An' now it's bloody murder, but all the while they
      'ear
'Is voice, the same as barrick drill, a-shepherdin'
      the rear.

'E's just as sick as they are, 'is 'eart is like to
      split,
But 'e works 'em, works 'em, works 'em till 'e
      feels 'em take the bit;
The rest is 'oldin' steady till the watchful bugles
      play,
An' 'e lifts 'em, lifts 'em, lifts 'em through the
      charge that wins the day!

The 'eathen in 'is blindness bows down to wood
      an' stone;
'E don't obey no orders unless they is 'is own;
The 'eathen in 'is blindness must end where 'e
      began,
But the backbone of the Army is the noncom-
      missioned man !

*Keep away from dirtiness — keep away from
    mess.*
Don't get into doin' things rather-more-or-less!
Let's ha' done with abby-nay, kul, an' hazar-ho;
Mind you keep your rifle an' yourself jus' so!

THE SHUT-EYE SENTRY.

Sez the Junior Orderly Sergeant
    To the Senior Orderly Man:
" Our Orderly Orf'cer's *hokee-mut*,
    You 'elp 'im all you can.
For the wine was old and the night is cold,
    An' the best we may go wrong,
So, 'fore 'e gits to the sentry-box,
    You pass the word along."

Then it was " Rounds!   What rounds?" at two
    of a frosty night,
  'E's 'oldin' on by the sergeant's sash, but, sentry,
    shut your eye.
An' it's "Pass! All's well!" Oh, ain't 'e rockin'
    tight!
  'E'll need an affidavit pretty badly by-an'-bye.

The moon was white on the barricks,
    The road was white an' wide,
An' the Orderly Orf'cer took it all,
    An' the ten-foot ditch beside.

An' the corporal pulled an' the sergeant pushed,
  An' the three they wagged along,
But I'd shut my eyes in the sentry-box,
  So I didn't see nothin' wrong.

Though it was "Rounds! What rounds?" O
  corporal, 'old 'im up!
'E's usin' 'is cap as it shouldn't be used, but,
  sentry, shut your eye.
An' it's "Pass! All's well!" Ho, shun the foam-
  in' cup!
'E'll need, etc.

'Twas after four in the mornin';
  We 'ad to stop the fun,
An' we sent 'im 'ome on a bullock-cart,
  With 'is belt an' stock undone;
But we sluiced 'im down an' we washed 'im
  out,
  An' a first-class job we made,
When we saved 'im smart as a bombardier
  For six o'clock parade.

It 'ad been "Rounds! What rounds?" Oh, shove
  'im straight again!
'E's usin' 'is sword for a bicycle, but, sentry, shut
  your eye.

An' it was "Pass!   All's well!"   'E's called me
        "darlin' Jane"!
  'E'll need, etc.

        The drill was 'ard an' 'eavy,
            The sky was 'ot an' blue,
        An' 'is eye was wild an' 'is 'air was wet,
            But 'is sergeant pulled 'im through.
        Our men was good old trusties—
            They'd done it on their 'ead;
        But you ought to 'ave 'eard 'em markin' time
            To 'ide the things 'e said!

For it was "Right flank—wheel!" for "'Alt, an'
        stand at ease!"
    An' "Left extend!" for "Centre close!" O
        marker, shut your eye!
An' it was, "'Ere, sir, 'ere! before the colonel
        sees!"
    So he needed affidavits pretty badly by-an'-bye.

        There was two-an'-thirty sergeants,
            There was corp'rals forty-one,
        There was just nine 'undred rank an' file
            To swear to a touch o' sun.

There was me 'e'd kissed in the sentry-box
 (As I 'ave not told in my song),
But I took my oath, which were Bible truth,
 I 'adn't seen nothin' wrong.

There's them that's 'ot an' 'aughty,
 There's them that's cold an' 'ard,
But there comes a night when the best gets
 tight,
 An' then turns out the Guard.
I've seen them 'ide their liquor
 In every kind o' way,
But most depends on makin' friends
 With Privit Thomas A.

When it is "Rounds! What rounds?" 'E's
 breathin' through 'is nose.
 'E's reelin', rollin', roarin' ripe, but, sentry, shut
 your eye.
An' it's "Pass! All's well!" An' that's the way
 it goes.
 We'll 'elp 'im for 'is mother, an' 'e'll 'elp us
 by-an'-bye.

14

"MARY, PITY WOMEN!"

You call yourself a man,
    For all you used to swear,
An' leave me, as you can,
    My certain shame to bear?
    I 'ear! You do not care—
    You done the worst you know.
I 'ate you, grinnin' there. . . .
    Ah, Gawd, I love you so!

Nice while it lasted, an' now it is over—
Tear out your 'eart an' good-bye to your lover!
What's the use o' grievin', when the mother that
        bore you
(Mary, pity women!) knew it all before you?

It aren't no false alarm,
    The finish to your fun;
You—you 'ave brung the 'arm,
    An' I'm the ruined one;

An' now you'll off an' run
    With some new fool in tow.
Your 'eart ?   You 'aven't none. . . .
    Ah, Gawd, I love you so!

When a man is tired there is naught will bind
    'im ;
All 'e solemn promised 'e will shove be'ind 'im.
What's the good o' prayin' for The Wrath to
    strike 'im,
(Mary, pity women !) when the rest are like 'im ?

    What 'ope for me or—it ?
    What's left for us to do ?
    I've walked with men a bit,
    But this—but this is you!
    So 'elp me Christ, it's true!
    Where can I 'ide or go ?
You coward through an' through! . . .
    Ah, Gawd, I love you so!

All the more you give 'em the less are they for
    givin'!
Love lies dead, an' you can not kiss 'im livin'.
Down the road 'e led you there is no returnin',
(Mary, pity women !) but you're late in learnin'.

You'd like to treat me fair ?
        You can't, because we're pore ?
We'd starve ?   What do I care!
        We might, but *this* is shore:
        I want the name—no more—
        The name, an' lines to show,
An' not to be an 'ore. . . .
        Ah, Gawd, I love you so!

*What's the good o' pleadin', when the mother
        that bore you*
(Mary, pity women!) knew it all before you?
Sleep on 'is promises an' wake to your sorrow,
(Mary, pity women!) for we sail to-morrow!

FOR TO ADMIRE.

THE Injian Ocean sets an' smiles
　　So sof', so bright, so bloomin' blue;
There aren't a wave for miles an' miles
　　Excep' the jiggle from the screw.
The ship is swep', the day is done,
　　The bugle's gone for smoke an' play;
An' black ag'in' the settin' sun
　　The Lascar sings, " *Hum deckty hai!* " *

　　For to admire an' for to see,
　　　　For to be'old this world so wide—
　　It never done no good to me,
　　　　But I can't drop it if I tried!

I see the sergeants pitchin' quoits,
　　I 'ear the women laugh an' talk,
I spy upon the quarter-deck
　　The orficers an' lydies walk.

---

* " I'm looking out."

I thinks about the things that was,
　An' leans an' looks acrost the sea,
Till, spite of all the crowded ship,
　There's no one lef' alive but me.

The things that was which I 'ave seen,
　In barrick, camp, an' action too,
I tells them over by myself,
　An' sometimes wonders if they're true;
For they was odd—most awful odd—
　But all the same now they are o'er,
There must be 'eaps o' plenty such,
　An' if I wait I'll see some more.

Oh, I 'ave come upon the books,
　An' often broke a barrick rule,
An' stood beside an' watched myself
　Be'avin' like a bloomin' fool.
I paid my price for findin' out,
　Nor never grutched the price I paid,
But sat in Clink without my boots,
　Admirin' 'ow the world was made.

Be'old a cloud upon the beam,
　An' 'umped above the sea appears
Old Aden, like a barrick-stove
　That no one's lit for years an' years!

I passed by that when I began,
    An' I go 'ome the road I came,
A time-expired soldier-man
    With six years' service to 'is name.

My girl she said, " Oh, stay with me! "
    My mother 'eld me to 'er breast.
They've never written none, an' so
    They must 'ave gone with all the rest—
With all the rest which I 'ave seen
    An' found an' known an' met along.
I cannot say the things I feel,
    But still I sing my evenin' song:

  For to admire an' for to see,
      For to be'old this world so wide—
  It never done no good to me,
      But I can't drop it if I tried!

·L'ENVOI·

WHEN Earth's last picture is painted, and the tubes
    are twisted and dried,
When the oldest colours have faded, and the
    youngest critic has died,
We shall rest, and, faith, we shall need it—lie
    down for an æon or two,
Till the Master of All Good Workmen shall set us
    to work anew!

And those that were good shall be happy: they
    shall sit in a golden chair;
They shall splash at a ten-league canvas with
    brushes of comets' hair;
They shall find real saints to draw from—Mag-
    dalene, Peter, and Paul;
They shall work for an age at a sitting and never
    be tired at all!

And only the Master shall praise us, and only the
Master shall blame;
And no one shall work for money, and no one
shall work for fame;
But each for the joy of the working, and each, in
his separate star,
Shall draw the Thing as he sees It for the God of
Things as They Are!

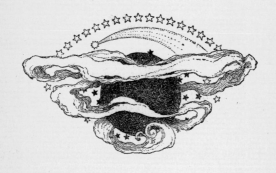

*T*HE BEGINNERS OF A NATION. A History of the Source and Rise of the Earliest English Settlements in America, with Special Reference to the Life and Character of the People. The first volume in A History of Life in the United States. By EDWARD EGGLESTON. Small 8vo. Cloth, gilt top, uncut, with Maps, $1.50.

It is nearly seventeen years since the studies for this book were begun. In January, 1880, having decided to write a History of Life in the United States, Mr. Eggleston employed himself during convalescence in seeking books bearing on the subject on all the quays of Paris. From that beginning has grown the large and valuable collection of many thousand books relating to American history, and to social, industrial, and intellectual life generally in the seventeenth and eighteenth centuries, which fill the walls of a stone library building on Lake George. Mr. Eggleston has produced, in the years since that beginning was made, two novels and several school-books on American history, now widely used; but eleven of the last seventeen years have been wholly given up to investigations and studies which find their first permanent result in the present volume. Thirteen articles on Colonial Life were contributed to the Century Magazine by the author between 1882 and 1889. They were recognized at once as authority on the subject, were quoted in learned works, were discussed by at least one scholar in a German periodical, were placed in class libraries in leading institutions of learning, and were cited by a well-known professor as "the only authority on colonial life to be depended on." Mr. Eggleston was importuned to gather them into a book, but his project had grown with his knowledge of the subject, and he has given himself of late years to produce on an entirely new plan the first of a series of volumes, each to be complete in itself, which as a whole shall represent the life of the people of the United States in the seventeenth and eighteenth centuries. In order to do this, it has been necessary not only to prosecute studies in most of the great public libraries of this country, but also to make repeated sojourns in Europe for the purpose of investigations in the British Museum and the State Paper Department of the Record Office, and the French National Library. Mr. Eggleston gained access also to papers not before used in private repositories in England and America. To get local color and additional information, he has visited all of the original thirteen colonies. The first installment of this historical series is thus the ripe fruit of many years of tireless investigation. The book has been wrought out and thought out thoroughly, and the initial stage of United States history is presented here in a light strangely different from that to which readers of history have been accustomed.

New York: D. APPLETON & CO., 72 Fifth Avenue.